Sketches of an Earlier Time

A Combat Veteran of Three Wars Recounts a Twentieth Century Life of Duty and Adventure

Colonel (Ret.) Scotty O. Ferguson

MERRIAM PRESS

HOOSICK FALLS, NEW YORK

2019

First published in 2018 by the Merriam Press

Second Edition

ISBN 978-0-359-74085-7
Library of Congress Control Number: 2018959947

This work was designed, produced, and published in
the United States of America by the

Merriam Press
489 South Street
Hoosick Falls NY 12090

E-mail: ray@merriam-press.com
Web site: merriam-press.com

The Merriam Press publishes new manuscripts on historical subjects, especially military history and with an emphasis on World War II, as well as reprinting previously published works, including reports, documents, manuals, articles and other materials on historical topics.

Contents

Foreword 5

Part 1: The Early Years 7

Part 2: World War II.. 21

Part 3: The Interim Years 59

Part 4: The Korean War 75

Part 5: The Cold War 95

Part 6: The Vietnam War 125

Part 7: The Later Years.. 135

Final Thoughts 141

Foreword

One day, sometime after I retired from the Air Force in 1975, a very large package was delivered to our door. It was from my sister. Between her and my mother, they had saved every letter, V-mail, and picture that my brother and I had sent them during our deployments in World War II. They had also saved many that I had sent from my time in the Korea and Viet Nam conflicts. There was a note inside the package that read, "Here's your book." That was meant, I presumed, to encourage me to sit down and chronicle those years. But for whom? There were thousands just like me who had similar experiences.

My early retirement years were interspersed with business endeavors, some commercial flying and lots of recreational activity. I was never bored, but never got around to writing "the book." The years passed too quickly, and my physical abilities have long since gone south. Then, in a recent year, just before Christmas, one of our adult granddaughters sent us a commercial memoir template, encouraging my wife Barbara and me to write our life stories for family posterity. The template style didn't appeal to me, but I finally sat down one day and just started writing.

The finished product was a series of vignettes from our earliest years growing up in the 1920s and 1930s until my retirement from the Air Force. Some who read the "grandchildren's version" of the memoir told us that others, outside the family, might also find it interesting to read, such as young Americans entering our military. For them, reading a true and highly personalized account of action in and between our major wars might provide a helpful perspective they would not get until they, too, are thrown into the middle of similar events and expected to perform, and survive. So, with the assistance of my children, we edited the original version to be more suitable for a broader readership and had it published.

My memory of those past events is, I think, quite accurate because they were just that – memorable. Most of our friends from our military days, and all the family members of our own generation are no longer with us to offer their own recollections into our shared pasts. So, this comes straight from the memory banks of my wife and me, and from what was kept in that box full of personal history that my sister mailed to me years ago.

This is a story of ordinary people living in extraordinary and dangerous times. We survived it. So many others did not. We dedicate our story to them, and to our future military veterans and their spouses.

Scotty Ferguson, May 2018

Part 1

The Early Years

I was born May 1, 1925, in a house my father built on a half-acre of land located in a small community southeast of Portland, Oregon, called Ardenwald. The house had four rooms: a kitchen with a wood burning stove; a living room, also with a wood burning stove; and two equal-sized bedrooms. That was it. The toilet (an outhouse) was several yards to the rear of the house. I had a sister (Betty), four years older, and a brother (Larry), two and a half years older. I was named Scotty Oren Ferguson. My first name tied me to the country of my grandfather's birth.

Life was hard on this half-acre of land. Perishable food was kept in an ice box. Wood had to be sawed and cut for cooking and heating. My brother and I did that using a regular logger's two-man crosscut saw. It was a learning process. The secret was, pull only, never push. Our father would have seasoned fir logs brought to the property by the cord. After the sawing came the splitting, which we did with a fallers axe. It had a long wood handle mounted in the center of two sharp metal edges. The wood had to be cut in two sizes, one size for the cook stove and a larger size for the heating stove. Finally, we had to stack it in a wood shed. Then there was the garden. One quarter of the land had to be cultivated to grow food. Spading one quarter of an acre with hand shovels was back-breaking. After the spading came the raking and finally the planting.

My father often referred to the property as, "Hell's half acre," but I have only good memories of our lives there. When our chores were done, we had plenty of space and time to play. Our imaginations were all we needed. Sometimes we were cowboys, or maybe we had a detective agency. We loved to follow the real action on the radio. I well remember hearing on a radio broadcast the day John Dillinger was killed, the most famous gangster at the time. It saddened us that the exciting stories about his exploits would now stop.

Boxing was big in those days, so naturally that's what my brother and I would be. Boxers. We saved our pennies until we amassed 187 of them. I can't say whether that was enough for a set of gloves; I think our dad probably had to chip in. In any case, we got the gloves. Boxing each other and some neighborhood kids developed skills that would come in handy later in life.

My father, Oliver Oren Ferguson, was a mechanic and heavy equipment operator. When work was scarce locally, we relocated to one of the many logging camps along Oregon's coastal range where he was employed as a crane operator, loading the harvested logs onto railroad flatcars. This happened a couple of times. First in 1928, when I was three years old, and again in 1931. Too young to remember the first logging camp experience, I have many fond memories of the second, a real adventure for young boys.

The camp was somewhere in Clatsop County near Clatskanie. We lived in a small wooden structure not unlike the house my dad built. There was no town as such, just a mess hall for the single loggers. The schoolhouse was one room with three or four rows of desks and an area to hang coats. The teacher's name was Miss Anderson, but we all called her Misserson. She taught grades one through eight in this small room. Her calm, sweet demeanor and patience are unforgettable. Outside, a short distance away, was the outhouse. If any of us kids felt the need, we raised either one or two fingers. I always wondered why the necessity to specify. Maybe time away. I don't remember ever seeing two fingers raised.

Activities outside of school were numerous and varied. There were no playgrounds, just the railroad running through the camp and the forest around us. It was a kid's paradise. We were never bored, partly because it was a dangerous area. And we did dangerous things. For example, empty rail flatcars passed through the camp at slow speed, heading out to the logging area for loading. These slow-moving flatcars were too tempting for two little boys to pass up. My brother and I would jump on, ride a ways, jump off, and run back to do it again. Somehow, our mother found out about it. Willow bushes were in abundance in this area. She used a switch from one of them on our rear ends to convince us never to do that again, and we never did. We also liked tying ropes under a railroad trestle, hanging onto the ropes and swinging out over deep canyons, then swinging back and dropping just in time to avoid smashing into the trestle. Another time, when we were out on one of the trestles, my brother tried to slide through the ties near the end of the bridge and got his head stuck. My sister solved the problem by stepping on his head and pushing him on through, dropping him to ground below. He lost some skin and blood, and never tried that again.

The trestles we played on were abandoned and had a lot of missing ties. We ran across the trestles playing tag and other games. In some areas, it was hundreds of feet to the bottom of the canyon. I don't remember anyone getting hurt, other than my brother Larry's skinned-up neck. We even built our own railroad. That is to say, the older kids built a railroad. It consisted of full-sized railroad track laid out maybe 75-100 feet, sloped up on one end and anchored with regular railroad spikes on full-sized ties. The engineer's compartment was built out of scrap wood. We would push it backward to the top of the sloped end, block the wheels, mount up, and then have the block knocked away from the wheel. On the roll-out, those left behind would jump on, just like real brakemen did in those days, and ride it to the stop. The end of the rails had a large plank nailed across to stop the "engine" from going off the track. This was our main toy.

The outlying areas of the camp were a young explorer's dream. There were streams for fishing with willow sticks fitted out with string, a hook and a worm; caves to explore; and hills to slide down. On one memorable occasion, I had run, jumped and slid down this hill when I heard a very loud growl. My brother ran down, grabbed me by the hair, and dragged me back to the top. Then we ran, never letting up until we were back inside our house. I will always believe my brother saved me that day from becoming lunch for a big, hungry bear.

One thing I never understood at the time was why we never had a gun of any kind in the house. For us, hunting was out of the question. Any venison we had, and we had a lot, was given to us by other loggers. I later found out why. My father was a soldier in a U.S. Army artillery unit in France during World War I and had witnessed too much killing. He was in the middle of the famous second battle of the Marne. He wouldn't even allow my brother or me to join the Boy Scouts. In any case, I can still remember the taste of wild venison. And the mince meat pies my mother made, mixing in left-over venison, were truly delicious and never duplicated, anywhere.

Some of our playmates at school were from families of foreign origin. My sister's best friend was from Japan, and my best friend was from Italy. When they left the camp they told us that their families were going back to their home countries. Later we wondered what role they played in World War II, and whether they had survived it.

Our second logging camp adventure ended abruptly when a forest fire broke out. The only way out was by rail, so that's how we left, with just the clothes we were wearing. My brother and I had to leave behind our scooters that we loved to ride, our first lesson in dealing with loss.

In 1932, after arriving back at the house in Ardenwald, I was seven years old and wanted a bicycle so bad I could taste it. My friend in our second-grade class had a new, red balloon-tire bike, the newest style on the market. Green with envy, I would have settled for any two-wheeler. One day, there it was. My father brought home a used bike he had picked up from who knows where. The economy was then in full depression, but when he was employed he made pretty good money. I suspect he bought the bike from someone who needed money for basics, like food to feed their family. We had a saxophone for a while that some-one had given as collateral for a loan, and later repossessed. I'm sure these kinds of personal loans among friends were common in those days because cash was precious, and trust was low.

Anyway, I now had my own bike, which made my sister and brother extremely jealous. When our mother was preoccupied and out of sight, they would tie me to a tree and leave me crying for release. But the bike was mine and I was on it a lot, mainly on the gravel street that ran in front of our house. One day the worst of the worst happened. A railroad main line ran several hundred yards to the west of our property where the road dead-ended. The speed limit on this gravel road was 25 MPH. I liked taking my bike up a steep driveway on the property west of ours, riding it fast downhill, breaking at the bottom and skidding around the corner. It didn't work out that way this time — I overshot the turn. At that instant, a car arrived at high speed traveling in the opposite direction. I was thrown into a culvert approximately 80 feet from impact, across the road and just west of our house. Our neighbor, who happened to be working on his car engine, got to me first and found that my right lower leg was broken in half – a compound fracture. He grabbed my leg with his greasy hands to stop the bleeding, which may have saved my life but also caused infection to set in. I was out of it. I don't remember anything but the pain. The first recommended course of action was amputation, which my parents rejected, insisting it be the very last resort. After my fifth operation and as many leg casts, I was finally on the mend. As for the cost of this medical care, I heard this story once from either my mother or sister. Our family doctor (who, incidentally, made many house calls) arranged for the leading bone specialist on the west coast to do all the operations. When the surgeon asked our doctor what he thought my parents could afford to pay, he told him "maybe 25 bucks." True? Maybe. Things like that happened in those times, quietly and privately. And, in all times, unforeseen circumstances alter the course of lives. In this case, my father had accepted a job offer in the San Francisco area just prior to my accident. He wouldn't leave due to my condition; the job was given to someone else, and that detour in our lives was never taken.

In 1936, we moved from the house in Ardenwald to a house in southeast Portland. It had four levels, an attic (scary place for an 11-year-old), a second floor with three bedrooms, a main level living area, and a spooky basement with a dirt floor. We still used wood for the kitchen stove and to fire the furnace in the basement, but now we had an indoor toilet and a real tub for bathing. And, we soon had a modern refrigerator. My father had a steady job, so things were looking up. I think my mother benefited the most from this sudden affluence. For instance, instead of doing the family laundry in a round, metal tub using a scrub board, she now had a new Maytag automatic washer.

This lifestyle change was dramatic, and traumatic, for a young boy, but it took only a short time to adjust. The changes came with higher living expenses, which required additional income. We all had to pitch in as best we could. I delivered papers and sold magazines door to door. Each fall, prior to the start of school, my mother would get us packed up, and off we would go to the hop yards near Salem, Oregon, employed as pickers for three weeks. It was there that I earned my first real money, $35, which I could spend on a brand-new bicycle. It was black and had a light, a horn, and brakes on both front and rear wheels. My new bike allowed me the freedom to get about with greater ease and regularity. Then one day, after a football game at the park, it was gone. Stolen! At that time, there were street gangs made up of the older, tougher types. We lived in the Woodstock neighborhood, so the one in our area was known, appropriately, as the Woodstock gang. They were also called the carline gang due to their propensity for boarding streetcars, tossing the conductor off, and driving it to their destination. I contacted a big Italian guy in this gang and told him someone had stolen my bike. He said, "Don't worry kid, we'll get it back for you." And he did, the next day. I never found out what happened to the thief, but I'm sure it wasn't pretty.

Since you have stayed with me this long, you have probably concluded that life in our early days was one hardship after another. In a sense it was, for most of society. But, unlike today, we were not constantly presented with contrasts between the economic classes. As kids, we enjoyed every minute of our busy lives, and we didn't depend on adults for guidance in the area of play. For example, Little League ball of any kind had not yet evolved. We formed our own teams and arranged competitive games against the kids in surrounding neighborhoods. So, how did mandatory adult supervision of kids' playtime come about? My theory is that when the World War II military masses were released back into American society, reproducing fast enough to offset the losses suffered during the great hate, they quite naturally maintained much of the disciplinary order drilled into their young, fertile minds. Therefore, their kids must be supervised as their First Sergeants or Chief Petty Officers did for them. Just a theory.

When I turned 16, I got my license to operate an automobile. This was no big deal to me since I had been able to drive since I was 10 or 11. My dad first taught me in a 1925 Dodge. Not that I drove a lot, but every chance he got he would put me in the driver's seat of whatever car we owned (and they were many and varied) for more instruction. In that same year, I bought my first car, a 1931 model-A Ford with a removable top and a rumble seat. It cost $100. My independence and maturity were growing. I could now accept work outside my immediate neighborhood, a necessity to meet the added expense I had assumed as proud owner of Henry Ford's finest. It was a momentous and happy time. It was May 1941. On December 7th of that year, all our lives would change dramatically.

Author after his bike accident.

Author on his tricycle, with brother Larry and sister Betty at logging camp.

The author's father, Oliver Ferguson, posing with his latest car.

SKETCHES OF AN EARLIER TIME

*The author's father, Oliver Ferguson,
in France as a soldier in World War I.*

Part 2

World War II

The war in Europe was expanding, and Japan was making life miserable for the Chinese. I paid little attention to these events until after the bombing of Pearl Harbor. My uncle, John Merryman, was living on Oahu with his family and working as a civilian engineer for the Navy department. During the Japanese air attack, he captured the entire event on his home movie camera. He subsequently turned the film over to the Navy for use by their intelligence personnel. The film was never returned to him.

Prior to the Pearl Harbor attack my brother Larry had joined the Army National Guard's 41st Infantry Division, which by then had been activated at Fort Lewis, located near Tacoma, Washington. My mother, sister and I drove there from Portland many times in my dad's latest car, a 1941 Ford, to visit him on weekends. It was a two-lane highway then, and sparsely populated along the way. Larry's time as an infantry soldier was short-lived. He had applied for schooling as an aviation cadet and was accepted for the training around mid-1942. His preliminary ground training courses took place at an Army camp in Santa

Ana, California. Shortly after he left for California, his infantry division was deployed to the Pacific theater where they would distinguish themselves as a great fighting force.

It is difficult to explain these times. The country was gearing up for a full-scale war effort. Everyone was aware. Right then my brother was part of it, and I wanted to experience it, too. So, I packed a few clothes in a bag, pocketed what money I had, and somehow got to Highway 99 South. From there, I hitchhiked my way to Santa Ana where I took up lodging in the local YMCA. I got a job working in a local liquor store advertised to have the largest wine stock in southern California. My glamorous duty was to keep dust off all the bottles. I would visit Larry at the camp on weekends, smuggling in liquor for him and his buddies. The store owner gave me the liquor after making me promise I wouldn't touch it myself.

While living at the YMCA I accepted any extra job that came along to supplement my meager income. One day I was asked if I could drive a truck. For extra money I would say yes to almost anything. The job was to transport all the camping equipment for a Girl Scout troop to their site in the San Bernardino mountains. The pay was five dollars. The truck had a high bed and was piled to the top with their equipment. I took off, figuring out the transmission gearing sequence as I went. As I neared the top of the first steep climb, the engine overheated and I had to pull off the road to let it cool. There was a rural store close by, which was fortunate because I had taken the cap off the radiator too soon, and the super-hot steam scalded my arm. I ran to the store and bought a tube of burn medicine for fifty cents. My pay had just shrunk 10 percent. I still needed water for the radiator, and I spotted a gas station just up the road. After the engine had cooled, I drove directly to the station for a radiator fill-up. As I drove in under the station overhang, I heard this loud crunch. I had caught the top of the truck bed on the overhang. The station attendant was an older mountain-man type. After he stopped ranting and raving over my faux pas, he asked what I needed. "Just a little water." To my surprise he let me fill up, and I was on my way. I arrived at the Girl Scout camp, delivered my cargo, and returned to Santa Ana a very experienced truck driver. My time there ended when my brother completed his training and left for primary flight school in Fort Stockton, Texas. I hitchhiked back to Portland.

A few weeks after returning home, I had saved enough money to buy a round-trip bus ticket to Fort Stockton for another visit with Larry. We were very close. What I didn't know was how long the trip would take. Automobile tires were made from rubber then, and the Japanese had taken over all the rubber tree plantations in the Pacific. Military vehicles had priority for what was available. Because of this, the national speed limit was 35 MPH. It took five days and five nights sleeping on the bus to get there, where I spent just one weekend. I met many interesting people, almost all of whom suggested that I return, finish high school, and take the exam for flight school. That didn't happen.

I turned 17 in May of that year. I talked with Melvin Chrisman, my friend since the sixth grade, about enlisting. At our age, we needed signed permission from our parents. Chances weren't good that my dad would sign a release after his experiences in World War I. So, we waited. At that time the Henry Kaiser Corporation was building cargo vessels (known as Liberty ships) at docks along the Willamette River in Portland. We both got work there as riveter's helpers. I was never sure how necessary this job was, but anything to speed up production and get supplies to the troops was worthwhile. Our pay was one dollar an hour, big money for both of us at the time. Melvin and I rode to work with an older gentleman who lived nearby and worked the same shift. Walking to his house one day for our ride, we saw a brand-new car sitting in his driveway: an Oldsmobile sedan. We were very much into cars in those days, so we were quite surprised to see no clutch on the driver's side. This was the first production-model passenger car with an automatic transmission. Impressive. Anyway, we worked at this job until the fall of 1942. On October 27th of that year, we both joined the Navy with our parents' reluctant permission. We boarded a train with many other recruits and headed for San Diego. On arriving, we were given a quick physical exam, a very short haircut, and assigned to quarters. Climbing up a stairway to my assigned space, some guy with a southern accent asked where I was from. When I replied "Portland, Oregon," he came back with "asshole of creation." I turned and hit him with a good right hook, dropping him to the bottom of the stairs. I never had any trouble with this guy again, or anyone else for that matter. Chalk it up to our early boxing practice as kids, and my general intolerance, even then, for jerks of any kind.

The training was intense. We used any off-duty time for personal upkeep. After six weeks we were either assigned to a permanent billet or sent off for further specialty training. Melvin went on to be stationed in Hawaii and remained there throughout the war. I was chosen to attend radio school there at the training station, which took another six to eight weeks. I wasn't happy about that because, at that age and given the circumstances, the war couldn't be won without me. Of course, I had no choice. I buckled down, learned the basics of the trade, and was finally reassigned. I transferred to the Terminal Island Naval Air Station near San Pedro, California, a few miles north, near Los Angeles. This was where pilots were trained to fly dive bombers, and where I experienced my first flight. One of the flight instructors took me up in a two-seat training plane with the designation SNJ, the Navy's version of the Army's T6 Texan. It was a wonderful introduction to the world of flight and a taste for what my brother Larry was doing at the time.

My primary duty as a radioman was to copy coded messages. Occasionally, one would come through in plain language. One Friday afternoon I copied a message originating on station. It stated, "Due to the continued unrest in and around the Los Angeles area, all personnel are restricted to base until further notice." It was Friday evening and I had plans for the weekend. My brother was now a 2nd Lieutenant fighter pilot, training in P-38s out of a base near Glendale, California. We were to meet there that evening. Shortly after receiving the message, I went off duty, ran to my quarters, grabbed my shaving kit, and ran fast for the front gate before the restriction was implemented. This was the reason for the restrictive order: a young Mexican man had raped a sailor's wife. The sailor found the man and killed him. Chaos broke out all over the area. For example, groups of off-duty sailors would enter theaters, get the lights turned on, grab any young Mexicans and beat them up badly. It got so bad that local police were known to have directed sailors to Mexican gang locations, then stand back and watch the fight. The Mexican gang types were easily identified. They wore knee-length jackets over pants which were pegged at the bottom, commonly known as "Zoot Suits." This was how the LA riots were identified all over the country. Anyway, after making it out of the gate just in time, I began hitchhiking toward Glendale. I was walking along an urban street looking for a ride when I noticed two black guys some distance behind me. I heard one yell, "Let's get the sailor!" I took

SKETCHES OF AN EARLIER TIME

off running. As they closed the gap, a big yellow school bus pulled alongside me with the door open. The driver yelled, "Jump in, sailor!" I did, and he closed the door and sped away. Close call. There were no students on board, so he drove me almost to my destination.

Larry and I met there several times. One time, we were in a bar and got into an argument, probably over a girl. We took it outside. After sparring around and throwing a few punches on the sidewalk, his landing more than mine, I heard someone shout, "Stop them, they're brothers!" Just then some guy stepped in to break us up. Larry stepped back, threw a quick right to the guy's jaw, and down he went. We then resumed throwing punches until the police arrived. The country was now at war big time, so incidents like these were not unusual, i.e., scuffles and routine stops by the police.

Later, in the fall of 1943, I received notice of transfer to a unit scheduled for overseas duty. I was finally going to war. The unit was located at the Tanforan horse racing track in the South San Francisco area. The track had been taken over by the government to house and train thousands of troops prior to deployment. Our temporary quarters had wooden floors and walls of thin paper over studs. Nights are chilly this time of year in the Bay Area, so keeping warm required ingenuity and midnight requisitions of the blanket supply. The training was conducted under cover of the race track grandstand and was more like a mini combat infantry course, i.e., care and use of the Garand rifle, technique for tossing grenades, hand-to-hand combat, etc.

As our departure date drew near, I submitted a request for a five-day leave. My brother was then stationed at Muroc Dry Lake (now Edwards AFB) out in the Mojave Desert, northeast of Los Angeles. He was there for P-38 gunnery training prior to his departure for Europe. My request was denied. I left anyway: AWOL. When I got into the area, I caught a ride with a local who drove me all the way out to the base. Driving through that barren desert, he pointed out this odd silhouette a mile or so dead ahead of us. It had the appearance of a battleship, and so it was, made of wire and wood. It was used as a target for skip-bombing practice by the P-38 pilots out of Muroc.

I was there for two nights before starting back. On the second night, I spent a lot of time in a bar near the base that had a large entertainment area. It was run by a woman named Poncho Barnes. She was a famous personality then, and even more so a few years later when she figured prominently in the life of Captain Chuck Yeager while he trained for his famous flight, breaking the sound barrier in the X-1 Rocket plane. My brother told me she brought in show girls who performed at the then famous Earl Carrol's Hollywood night club. They were all gorgeous and tall, a requirement of the job. Accompanied by a big band, he said they put on a great show.

I left the following day, hitchhiking my way back to face whatever punishment I was due for my unauthorized departure. It was mid-November 1943. I got back just in time. We were scheduled to board a ship, tied up at a dock in San Francisco Bay, in just a few days. My unauthorized leave was recorded, and that was it. We packed our sea bags early one cold November morning and took buses to the San Francisco waterfront. We boarded the M.S. Day Star, a Norwegian vessel manned by a civilian Norwegian crew and contracted by the U.S. government for just such purposes. Our sleeping area consisted of row after row of hanging canvas hammocks, six high. Separation was narrow, so take your choice — sleep belly down or belly up. As we went aboard in single file, a crew member would take our sea bags and toss them down an open hatch. We would later collect them after being assigned our sleeping areas. I will always remember the guy ahead of me. Just as they started to throw his sea bag toward the hatch, he screamed, "No, no, no!" When it hit the deck below, the sound of shattering glass told the story. His attempt to smuggle several bottles of booze aboard had just failed miserably.

Passing under the Golden Gate Bridge and reaching open water, the excitement mounted. We were a boatload of mostly teenagers, most of whom had never been very far from their childhood neighborhoods. Cruising westward and watching San Francisco fade out of sight, I'm sure most of us were thinking: Will we ever see it again? Those feelings soon passed as we became accustomed to routine life aboard ship. We were gradually given more information about the voyage, but nothing about the destination. For example, we were told we were running a zigzag course due to the enemy submarine threat, which resulted in an average forward speed of a blazing nine knots per hour. It was going to take some time to cross this big ocean.

A major task aboard ship was upkeep of ourselves and our personal items. For example, there were no toilets or showers available for troop use. In place of toilets was a metal half-round arrangement that ran from one side of the ship to the other, taking in sea water at one end and emptying it out at the other. Squatting over it with all the company around you took a while to get used to. Showers were taken on the top deck whenever we had a good rain. We learned a few tricks from one old sailor, like how to clean our dungarees. You would tie a small line around them, tie the other end to any stationary object on the deck, throw them overboard, and let the ocean do the rest. It worked great if you didn't forget and leave them there too long.

We were hungry all the time. Our main meal was typically one Spam sandwich, no seconds. And then came Thanksgiving of the year of our Lord 1943, a day that will not be forgotten in my lifetime. The aromas coming from the galley were so different, we knew something gastronomically great was about to happen. As we passed through the chow line, there it was, mounds of roast turkey with all the trimmings. We piled our tin plates high with all the goodies in sight. That night we hit the sack with full, contented stomachs for the first time since we lost sight of the City by the Bay. Then it started. I awoke with bad stomach cramps. I wasn't alone. Bodies were crammed together along the toilet trough. As one got up, another immediately took his place, but that trough would handle only so many bodies at a time. Hence, 'IT' was everywhere, including the top deck where many of the troops had gone in their attempt to hang it over the side. By morning the worst was over, and the cleanup, which seemed insurmountable, began. All decks, ladders, gunwales: everything had to be hosed down, hand-scrubbed and hosed down again. It took two days before we returned to our normal shipboard routine.

Entertainment aboard this vessel was mostly left to our own devices. There were no movies, and not much of anything to read. One day the second in command (the First Mate) — who incidentally looked exactly like Douglas Fairbanks Jr, a major movie star of the day — came out on the bridge and announced that anyone interested could sign up for boxing matches to be held the following day on the aft upper deck. They were to be three-round matches, with the winners receiving a carton of cigarettes. Being a smoker and low on supply, I signed up. While I was sitting next to the ring watching one of the matches, I overheard a nearby conversation that went like this: "Who are you fighting today?" "Some guy named Ferguson." "How do you think you'll do?" "Well, I won my weight in the Golden Gloves fights in New York; shouldn't be a problem." Uh-oh, I thought. I'm in trouble. When we climbed into the ring that day and exchanged the first few punches, I realized that this guy was a talker, not a boxer. I easily won all three rounds and my carton of cigarettes. I silently gave thanks for all those hours of childhood boxing.

Another memorable day aboard this ship occurred when we crossed the equator. Formal initiation for sailors crossing this imaginary line for the first time is a centuries-old custom. The old salts had rigged up as bad a torture chamber as they could. They constructed a canvas tunnel with sea water rushing through it. All of us first-timers had to enter the tunnel and crawl through the rushing water to the other end while being beaten through the wet canvas with oars or whatever they could get their hands on. When the ceremony was complete, we were issued a card stating that we had been duly initiated into the Solemn Mysteries of the Ancient Order of the Deep. I still have that card.

We had been at sea for more than a month, depending only on Mother Nature for an occasional respite from the daily norm. Spotting dolphin and flying fish had become routine. Land – that's what we wanted to see. Then one morning there it was, off on the distant horizon. Australia. We watched that spot of land get larger and larger for most of the day until we reached a point off the city of Townsville and dropped anchor. The ship's captain and the senior military officer went ashore, we assumed to receive orders for our final destination. It turned out to be New Guinea, a very large island not far from and east of Australia. We weren't informed of this until we arrived there, 42 days after leaving San Francisco.

We disembarked in New Guinea in an area known as Milne Bay, which had long since been swept clean of enemy forces by Australian and U.S. Army forces. Our mission was to set up an amphibious base for small boat operations in support of the larger effort, both in logistics and my area, communications. We were set up in temporary quarters until our permanent area of operations was completed at Stringer Bay. The whole area surrounding us was swarming with activity. Cargo ships moved in and out, aircraft engines of all types made constant sounds, and construction noise could be heard in all directions.

Until we were set up for doing our thing, we had to be kept busy. This meant manual labor on the waterfront transferring dry goods, fruits and vegetables, electronics, etc., from the dock to small boats for delivery to units around the bay. Since a lot of us were teenagers and hungry most of the time, we would sample almost anything edible that we handled. One day we were working with tons of fresh pineapple, and we gorged on it. Big mistake. To this day I am not a fan.

New Guinea was like no place I'd ever known. During some rare off-time, several of us decided to explore the immediate jungle behind us. For some reason, I had to delay and catch up with the group later. As I progressed through the thick jungle I came upon a fast-moving stream. I thought, Can I jump? Or, should I take off my boots and wade across? When I looked to the other side, I froze. There stood a very large lizard, three to four feet long with a dinosaur profile. It was the ugliest creature I had ever seen. It probably thought the same of me as we both turned and ran in opposite directions. I later described the animal to an English-speaking native. His reaction: "No big animals here, only big animals in America." Apparently, he had never heard of Africa.

After finally settling into our permanent area of operations and the routine of life in New Guinea, the heat and constant humidity began to wear. The war was moving north of us at a rapid pace, so much so that we were finding it difficult to maintain adequate food supplies. This forced us to become hunters and gatherers. The Army troops around us formed hunting parties. They brought in wild boar, penned them in, and butchered them as needed. They tasted quite good.

One day a group of Naval officers came to our unit looking for volunteers to form a new type of combat unit called beach parties, an innocuous name with a dangerous mission. The mission was to accompany the first wave of a landing force onto a beach, then coordinate the landing of the following forces until all men and materials were ashore. This could take days, which meant our training, to include basic infantry knowledge, would be intense. We were all interviewed individually. Only one question still sticks with me to this day. With a stern look on his face, my interviewer asked, "Does it scare you when bombs go off?" My quick answer was, "I have no idea. I've never heard one go off." I wondered if this was why I was chosen.

We were formed into three units consisting of 19 men and three officers, designated Beach Party Numbers 4, 5 and 6. I was assigned to Number 4. One of our officers was a medical doctor, probably in his forties. Our commanding officer was a Navy lieutenant named Zinzer, so it seemed natural to call ourselves Zinzer's Raiders. Our training began immediately in the local area. First it was firearms: the Garand infantry rifle, Thompson sub-machine gun, and the Carbine. Since I would be responsible for the communications, carrying a portable radio on my back and using semaphore flags, I chose the lighter, less bulky Carbine. We were training for a specific mission, but we knew not where. Then the travel began. Oddly enough, the first ship we boarded was a Chinese cargo vessel. It took us north to somewhere around Lae, New Guinea, where we disembarked and later boarded an Australian troop ship. The plan was to disembark the troops over the side using rope ladders, then into waiting landing craft, and from there to the beachhead. We practiced this a lot.

We stayed aboard this vessel maybe two weeks. The food was awful. Most breakfasts consisted of tripe on stewed tomatoes, with tea. I looked forward to the four o'clock bell every day, which meant tea time. Cookies went with tea time. That's how I survived. Forget the tea. I hate tea to this day. The Australian crew was nice enough, but they used the foulest language in a normal conversation I'd ever heard.

The constant sweating during the training in this tropical climate began to take a toll on my vulnerable pale skin. I broke out in a heat rash from head to toe. It was irritating and painful. Anything I tried for relief failed. What I didn't know was that a cure for my condition would soon be available. In any case, it became apparent that this method of transporting and landing the troops at our scheduled destination was being abandoned. We were then transported to another area of New Guinea known as Finschhafen. Our unit disembarked and set up camp in the foothills of the Owen Stanley Mountain range. We strung up jungle hammocks equipped with mosquito nets, near a beautiful waterfall. It was a double waterfall with flowers, even wild orchids, growing all around the area. Each waterfall created a deep blue pool. The beauty of the place was indescribable. After setting up camp, we headed directly to the falls. After a few hours in that cold fresh water, my heat rash disappeared completely. Life was good again.

After just a couple of days there we were recalled to duty. Training was over. The decision had been made as to how we would deploy. We were taken aboard a vessel none of us had ever heard of: the designation was LSD or Landing Ship Dock. The name on the bow and stern of the ship was Gunston Hall. It was a unique kind of ship in that it was literally a dock. The aft end would be flooded to allow landing craft to enter under power, align for exit, and shut down their engines before pumping the water back out. We joined a very large task force consisting of troop carriers, cruisers, destroyers, LSTs, the works. We were far out to sea with no land in sight. There were ships in any direction one looked. The destroyers would weave through the convoy, occasionally dropping a depth charge off their stern because of a possible submarine detection. It was especially dramatic observing the explosion on the surface of the ocean.

By now we had learned which Army unit we would be working with. To my surprise, it was part of the same unit my brother had been with in Tacoma, Washington — the 41st Infantry Division. They were probably the most famous fighting force in the Pacific theater. During the battle of Salamaua, New Guinea, they spent 75 straight days fighting from foxholes, killing more Japanese than the Marines did during the entire battle for Guadalcanal. It was good to know we would be working with the best.

We received our final briefing D minus one. We would be landing on a beach of Humboldt Bay in the area of Hollandia, Dutch New Guinea, going in with the first three waves. It is located close to the center of the northern coast of New Guinea.

That night one of the worst things that could happen, happened. We were all hanging around on the upper deck chatting or just being alone with our personal thoughts when a tremendous explosion occurred somewhere on the same deck. It turned out that one soldier, for some unknown reason, had pulled the pin on a hand grenade. While trying to replace the pin, he dropped the grenade. No one grabbed it and tossed it overboard; they all just dove for cover. I never found out how many were hit by shrapnel, but I know that one sailor, a member of the ship's crew, took the brunt of the blast. I will mention more about this individual later, but this incident demonstrates that even in the best units there can be at least one dumbass. On the bright side, I remember talking that night with a couple of the 41st's best about their plans for the next day. They explained how they had rigged their LCM with rocket launchers along both gunnels, so they could take care of any Japanese ships they came across. I found out later that they did encounter one and sank it.

I don't remember sleeping much that night. We were up early, dressed, packed and ready. H hour was 7:00 a.m. We made our way aft and down to the boats. It was dark as pitch in there.

The boats were banging into each other as we moved to our assigned landing craft. It was truly a wonder that someone didn't get an arm or a leg smashed in that chaos. Yet, all went well. We departed at the designated time and headed out to our orbit point. Meanwhile, a devastating sea and air bombardment was taking place. Shells fired from the warships behind us were coming in over our heads. Navy dive bombers were pulling up overhead after dropping bombs on targets a short distance inland. When the pre-invasion action finally ended, we were given the signal to start in for the beach. That's when we started taking artillery rounds. We could see the flashes from the shore and the explosions in the water around us. The cruiser Phoenix then took action, pulling in between us and the shore battery and letting go with a full broadside blast that quickly took care of the problem.

As we continued in toward the beach with LCMs staggered in long lines, the pucker factor grew far beyond anything I had ever experienced. This was the real thing and there was no escape, like closing your eyes in a movie. The large ramp on the LCM obscured any vision straight ahead. When I felt the bottom of the boat start scraping sand and saw the ramp drop, I expected the worst. It didn't happen. I saw one dead soldier, but that was it. Where was the enemy? It turned out that the pre-invasion deceptive tactics worked so well that only a small cadre of Japanese fighting troops remained in the Hollandia area. Thanks to the brilliant thinking and planning by General MacArthur and his staff, it went like this: The entire task force held a steady course toward the Wewak area, which was home base for a large Japanese fighting force. Thinking we would hit Wewak, they made the decision to pull their major fighting forces out of Aitape and Humboldt Bay and amass them all back at Wewak. It worked.

So, there we were on the beach looking for a good spot to dump our gear. Before that, we had to dig foxholes for cover. A couple of us found one that had already been dug for us by the Japs. We claimed it by throwing all our gear in, then went to work. Our main task was to mark the beach area for bringing in the large LSTs and establishing contact with the fleet of ships offshore. Communications was my job, which meant I had to stay right on the heels of the beach master.

That day we brought in at least eight LSTs loaded with an occasional tank and bulldozer, but mostly with ammunition of all types. Shortly after the initial landing we discovered a massive swamp 50 to 100 yards inland. It wasn't deep water, but the wet conditions prevented us from immediately dispersing the ammunition to an area away from the main body of troops. Late that afternoon, General MacArthur came ashore to discuss the situation with the 41st Division's General Krueger. This was historic to me because, as an 18-year-old, I'm standing with the beach master, privy to the entire discussion. At that time, General MacArthur was one of the most famous men on the planet.

That evening, as darkness began setting in and activity turned to personal necessities, I jumped into our large Jap-constructed foxhole, laid down my backpack radio, took off my boots and socks to let them dry out, and opened a k-ration for a quick bite. Then it happened: a massive explosion. The concussion threw several nearby soldiers in on top of me. It seemed like at least eight because I had such a tough time crawling up and out of there. A Japanese Betty bomber had dropped its bombs directly onto their own abandoned ammo dump, which in turn began igniting our ammo that was spread all down the beach. My only thought was to get away from the nearby constant explosions. Metal was flying everywhere just above the ground, making every type of sound imaginable. Each explosion sounded worse than the last. I was running away from sound and diving into any hole I came upon. It seemed impossible to escape. I remember hearing a medic very close by screaming for water while he took care of one of the wounded. I reluctantly pushed my canteen up above the hole I was in, hoping I wouldn't lose my arm from a piece of flying metal. He immediately grabbed it and went to work on the guy. (I found out later that our doctor, who was tending to one of the wounded, took a piece of flying metal in his rear end.) As the explosions became more intense, the next thing I remember was a bulldozer driver lowering his blade and heading directly into this holocaust of fiery explosions ... and disappearing, becoming part of the firestorm.

Finally, there came a lull. I hear this infantry lieutenant yelling that he needs people. He points to me and several others, directing us to stay with a sergeant who was standing in a foxhole, and with another soldier manning an anti-aircraft gun pointed not toward the sky, but level, toward the swampy area. He told us the Japs had landed south of us and would probably be coming at us through the swamp. Since I was unarmed, my carbine long since blown to bits back at my old foxhole, the sergeant hands me a grenade. There I am, expecting hand-to-hand combat, with a knife still strapped to my belt and one hand grenade. I stayed that way through most of the night, relieving myself in my helmet and throwing it out of the foxhole. Finally, we got the message that it was native canoes that had been spotted landing, not Japanese. Big relief, but not long afterwards the explosions started again, and the running for cover and jumping into holes. The final hole I jumped into had a board with a nail sticking through it. I hit that nail dead center into my bare foot. Now I was crippled, and I eventually had to be evacuated out to an LST hospital ship. General Eichelberger, I Corps Commander, and Admiral Barbey, 7th Amphibious Fleet Commander (with their driver) took me out in their personal LCVP to the hospital ship. As I was climbing up the rope ladder, one-legged style, I turned to wave and saw them both, standing and saluting.

Here's how that night's activity was described by an observer aboard a vessel offshore: "The holocaust on White Beach as viewed from the sea was so awesome and terrifying as to almost defy description. Great billowing black clouds of smoke were flung thousands of feet into the air from exploding drums of gasoline, while the oil, lubricant, rations, vehicles, and hundreds of tons of miscellaneous stores and gear burned below in a solid, hideous, frightening wall of flames five hundred feet in the air for a mile and a half along the beach. Through this dense pall of smoke and flame all kinds of ammunition set up a pyrotechnic display to end all boyhood impressions of Fourth of July fireworks. The spitting, vicious cackle of millions of rounds of small arms ammunition, grenades, and engineer's explosives permeated with increasing waves of sound the shattering, crashing, crumbling roar and rumble of barrage after barrage of heavy artillery shell. In all directions, in all colors of the rainbow, rockets, signal flares, and white phosphorous shells sprayed out...The fierce eerie glare made faces look green in the half light." And that's the way it was. Who knows how any of us survived.

After climbing aboard the hospital vessel, I was assigned a bunk directly across from a severely wounded soldier. He had a badly burned optic nerve and was in so much pain, he would scream and then pass out. He had to be strapped to his bunk to keep from falling out. A medic came through the area taking names of the wounded for submission for the award of Purple Hearts. When he came to me, I said, "Give mine to him," pointing to the guy who had just passed out.

That evening the LST beached to take on more wounded. I hobbled out to the bow to watch the action on the beach and saw an amazing sight. Our infantry troops were escorting several prisoners down the beach. One of them was a beautiful woman dressed in a long, flowing skirt. I thought, "Hey, I'm dreaming here." I found out later that this woman and some of the others she was with had been taken prisoner somewhere in China.

We departed the Hollandia area the following morning. Some of us were taken off ship at Finschhafen to a field hospital set up in a Quonset hut. This is where I found out about the sailor on the LSD who had taken most of the blast from the hand grenade that went off on the deck of the ship. He said they had removed over a hundred tiny pieces of metal from his back. Another sailor in this makeshift hospital with whom I had become friends was in real bad shape. He was a crew member on the Navy's version of the B-24 bomber that was shot down. After spending many days on a raft at sea, his wounds and exposure had proved too much. I came back from lunch one day and he was gone. While still there, I had a strange feeling come over me about the welfare of my brother in Europe, a feeling that all was not well.

Still without shoes on my feet, I was transported back to our rear area at Milne Bay. The first thing I did was check my mail. Among the assortment were V-mails that I had sent to my brother, with some sort of scribbling across them. I took them to the guy handling the mail. He said, "That says missing." I was devastated. Then I immediately felt my mother's deepening grief. Her youngest brother had been killed in action during a battle in the Italian campaign for which he received the nation's second highest award, the Distinguished Service Cross.

When the rest of our beach party arrived back at the rear base, I received more bad news. It seems that one of our guys had to use the latrine area in the middle of the night. Our man on guard duty who was holding a Thompson sub-machine gun didn't know he had left. So, when he returned to our foxhole area, the guard challenged him. At that same moment, the man stumbled, falling forward as if throwing a grenade. The guard fired. A round hit him in one shoulder and then came out through his other shoulder. That brought our tally to one dead and two wounded.

Our next combat operation took us north of Hollandia to an area called Sansapor. The objective was to occupy and establish an Army Air Corps fighter base on a nearby offshore island called Middleburg. We went in with the 24th Infantry Division. After months of training in Hawaii, this was to be their first taste of combat. Little or no opposition was expected upon initial landing. We were transported over choppy seas via LCI or Landing Craft Infantry. These were large round-bottomed vessels that pitched and rolled in any slight sea disturbance. One can imagine how it feels to be sick and throwing up just before running ashore on your first combat landing. It happened here.

As expected, the landing was unopposed. Most Japanese fighting forces had been evacuated, but not all. Our infantry rounded up approximately 120 prisoners. A large wire pen was constructed to hold them. They were given cans of C-rations but had no clue how to open them, cutting themselves in trying. Once our soldiers showed them the trick, a new problem arose. Since we were expecting air raids from Japanese bases on Biak Island northwest of us, our soldiers went into the prisoner enclosure to hand out shovels to the prisoners so they, too, could dig foxholes. Then the crying and wailing started. Someone eventually figured out why. They thought they were digging their own graves. One infantryman demonstrated the reason for digging the hole. He would point to the sky and yell, "Boom! Boom!" and then jump into the hole. It was quite an act, but he got the point across.

We depended on the units we landed with for incidentals, if you can call food an incidental. This infantry unit wasn't exactly generous with their rations. After a day or two, I volunteered to get us something to stop the growling in our stomachs. I went aboard one of the LSTs we had earlier directed ashore, climbed up a ladder to one of the upper decks, and found a sailor who volunteered to get me something to take back to our group. It turned out to be a whole sack of candy bars. On the way out of the ship I slipped going down a ladder to the lower deck. With my arms full of candy bars which I wasn't about to release, I hit face down on the steel deck. A sailor nearby called a medic who took a quick look at my smashed nose and told me to hold still while he manipulated the bones back into their original positions. He then put a piece of tape across the swollen area to hold everything in place. I thanked him and went on down the beach. When I got back and laid the booty down, they all said the obvious, "What the hell happened to you?" "I had to fight them for it," I said, as convincingly as possible.

I don't remember whether at Sansapor or Hollandia, but at one end of the beach there was a half-sunken Japanese barge of some sort. To bring landing craft onto the beach near it, we had to know whether it was on the bottom or floating freely. Before diving in and determining that it was floating freely, I took off my clothes down to my shorts and stacked them neatly up next to the thick jungle. When I went back to get my clothes, I grabbed a cigarette out of my shirt. As I was lighting it, I felt, and then heard, a presence behind me. I turned. There stood a native man and a young boy, both with wild hair and wearing loin cloths. The man pointed toward my cigarette pack and then to himself. I gave him one. He pointed toward the pack again, then to the boy, so I gave him one, too. They left and disappeared into the jungle. By then the hair on the back of my neck was beginning to lay down.

One dark night in Sansapor I was sitting on a log in the latrine area with a churning stomach when the first air raid alert was passed along. Everyone ran for their foxholes – everyone but me, that is. I'm stuck on a log in the jungle, in the pitch black, unable to move anywhere. "What a way to go," I thought. Fortunately, whatever was up there passed us by. On another day, several of us were swimming out to a PT boat anchored offshore. As we got close, we could see crew members standing on deck with rifles. They yelled that they were shooting at a crocodile. We must have set Olympic records swimming back to shore.

Middleburg Island was taken without resistance, but one infantry Captain was reported killed in action. This mystery was not solved while we were there, and probably never was.

We departed Sansapor aboard an LST and beached back at Hollandia of all places. That night the Bob Hope show was performing for the troops. It was quite good. I remember one of our guys saying, "We just took this place and all we get is rear seats." Actually, there were no seats, just logs laid down in rows. We stood behind the "non-combatants" as we called them, quite proud of ourselves now that we had participated in and survived two major operations. We left there on a troop ship the following day for transport back to Milne Bay. During this trip I had developed an excruciatingly painful ear ache. A doctor on board had me lie on a table. We were in quite heavy seas, so he had to time the roll of the ship to cut the abscess as we reached the top of a swell, before the ship plunged back down again. Very tricky, but it worked. The pain was gone immediately.

After a couple of days in Milne Bay, Zinzer got us together and told us that we would be getting an R&R to Australia. Our passage on a transport ship to Brisbane was over the Coral Sea, always rough. I have never been seasick, and I always loved this kind of sea. In fact, I loved getting up just under the covering at the bow of the ship and watching the foamy water splash over the top of me. Others weren't so fortunate. The gunnels were lined with guys vomiting over the side. I took advantage, asking a few of them if they were going to use their lunch chits. They would hand them to me as they threw up over the side, again. Unsympathetic, and profitable: one more spam sandwich. The ones who weren't continually nauseous on this trip would play poker below decks in our sleeping quarters, using Australian currency. Each bill denomination had a different color, so that's how we bet, by color, and quickly lost track of how much we were winning or losing.

We arrived at the port in Brisbane, grabbed our gear, disembarked, got a taxi and headed for a hotel. The military demand for gasoline was so great that civilians had to come up with a different way to fuel their vehicles. This was the first shock of our R&R. They used steam. To generate it, they burned coal in an enclosure in the vehicle's trunk to heat the water.

After only a day in Brisbane, we boarded a train headed for Sydney. It took most of the day to get there. We rented a flat in an area known as Kings Cross. The Australian Army took an awful beating, losing entire divisions of men during the initial phase of the New Guinea campaign. As a result, the young male population was scarce. I ran into this situation while having breakfast at a café in Sydney. An elderly lady came over to me, knowing by my Navy uniform that I was an American. She began chewing me out for the death of her son, a Lieutenant Commander in the Australian Navy. The owner of the café escorted her away from my table and then explained the reason for her anger. Her son had been aboard a Japanese prison ship when it was sunk by an American submarine. All on board were lost.

We all had a wonderful time enjoying all the fruits of civilization again. And then my luck ran out. In Australia, vehicles drive on the left side of the street. It was dusk, and I had had a couple of potent Aussie beers. Standing outside on a curb, I looked the wrong way before stepping off and was hit by a car, a U.S. Navy car. They took me to an American Navy hospital just outside Sydney. I suffered a green tree fracture of my right leg. The following day, all the guys from the beach party came to see me with the news that we had been recalled — our leave cut short — for a new combat operation. It turned out to be the invasion of Leyte Gulf. All the enlisted guys of our beach party came back to the hospital ward for a farewell visit prior to heading back to the combat zone for their next encounter with Japan's finest. They walked in half boozed up, with some accompanied by female companions. One of the ladies came up to my bed, lifted up her skirt and said, "Look, we traded skivvies." Sure enough, she had on U.S. Navy issued undershorts. I assumed our intrepid warrior was wearing hers. They all left after a short time, leaving me to explain their deportment. Most of my fellow patients were young combat veterans, so really, little explanation needed.

When hospitalized after combat, a lovely nurse couldn't help but cheer you up. A beautiful nurse, probably in her early twenties, was on our ward. Each time she entered she would cause an avalanche of rustling sheets from the simultaneous turning of bodies, just to get a glimpse. As my leg healed and the cast came off, massage of the muscle was prescribed to help return it back to normal. On my lucky days, she would perform this task, perfunctorily and without emotion, as a true medical professional. However, being a 19-year-old combat veteran and full of myself, I figured she would eagerly accept my romantic advances. During one of these massage sessions late in the evening, with a bright moon shining through the window, I came up with this great line: "Don't you think the moon looks beautiful tonight?" "It looks awfully damn cold to me," she replied. The damper was closed, the fire was out.

I knew I would soon be going back to my original unit at Milne Bay. Before that happened, I figured, why not ask for a few days leave? I had only used up a couple of days of my original leave prior to the accident; surely, I deserved it. My thinking, not theirs. I was turned down. I thought, "These clowns are sitting here in this paradise without hearing a shot fired in anger, and they're telling me I'm crowding their space. No way. I'm taking a few days." So, I did, then turned myself in to the shore patrol in Sydney. This turned out to be an adventure of its own. The Navy had taken over a small jail facility on the shore of Sydney harbor. It had a small office for the Marine guards, a prisoner compartment with bunk beds, a small open toilet and a shower area. That was it. We were crowded in there. Not long after I was brought in, I was abruptly woken one night with a man's fingers around my neck, choking me and screaming, "You stole my gin you son-of-bitch." A couple of the other guys jumped out of their bunks and pulled him off me. It turned out that this sailor had been AWOL four months and intoxicated the entire time. Now he was in the throes of severe delirium tremens (DTs). I didn't sleep well until this clown finally settled down.

And then there was the guy who was about to be released. A guard came in and told him, "Get your gear together, you're going back."

He replied, "To America?"

"No, you dumb shit," the Marine replied, "you're going back to New Guinea."

Another time, one of the prisoners was moaning and carrying on about how bad he felt. The guard called for a medic. He came in, took his temperature and, sure enough, it was high. They escorted him to an ambulance for transport to a medical facility. We were informed that he had escaped enroute. One of the prisoners told this story: The escaped prisoner had held a bar of soap under his arm long enough to drive up his temperature, and the rest is history. I have never checked to see if this armpit trick actually works.

After a short period of time, I was transferred by train to another jail in Brisbane. This procedure was a shocker. I was handcuffed with my legs chained and taken well-guarded to the train station. I remained in that condition for the entire trip. My thoughts were, I was AWOL, not a bank robber. They put me into a cell with another prisoner whose infraction of the rules I never learned. That night in our cell we discovered we had company, lots of company. The cell was infested with bed bugs. We stripped the covers off our mattresses and pulled them on and up to the tops of our heads, trying in vain to keep the bugs off our bodies. It was a sleepless night. I was released the next morning and escorted aboard a transport ship headed for New Guinea. It was Christmas day, 1944. When I arrived, I immediately went to see a friend who handled all the personnel records. He came up to me, and before I could say a word, he held up both arms and said, "Don't worry about it. Your files are clear of anything that may have happened in Australia." The troops are close in time of war; they look out for each other's welfare, no matter what.

Sometime in early 1945, our unit was moved to Subic Bay on Luzon, Philippine Islands. We set up an amphibious base there, doing real hard manual labor in stifling humidity. One day during this period, a friend and I confiscated a command car. It was like a big four-wheel drive convertible sedan. We drove through an area called the Zig Zag Pass to the city of Manila. The Pass was littered with burned out tanks and other vehicles, both Japanese and American. The sight of this major city was unreal. Bullet-riddled streetcars still sat on their tracks. All the buildings showed signs of the mauling they had taken from the battle action. Devastation was everywhere. We did manage to find a bar that was open and doing business, proving that a determined entrepreneur can be successful anywhere. Rum was all they had. We bought some and took it back through that wild pass, much to the joy of our buddies.

Compared to my last assignment, life in Subic Bay was quite mundane. My primary duty was in the radio shack, copying and delivering coded messages. Also, the surroundings, including the native population, were quite different. First of all, there were women. In New Guinea, we never saw one. Most natives spoke English, albeit broken, and they would barter to buy or sell anything. I was trying to buy a bracelet for my niece. When we finally agreed on a price, I called her a little gangster. She replied, calling me a p--king Jew. They couldn't pronounce the letter F.

At Subic I was assigned an additional duty. All personal mail still required censoring prior to posting. This was strictly officer's duty, but since the job became too much for the number of officers we had, a few enlisted personnel had to be selected. I was one of them. At first it bothered me to read the thoughts and actions of guys just like me being conveyed to their homefolks. Those feelings subsided after a while, and it got to be routine between the few of us to share the most bizarre portions of a letter. Intimate thoughts were pretty much ignored unless, to our young minds, they were super unusual. I remember yelling out, "Hey, did you know we were bombed last night?" In many letters, exaggeration was not unusual, and some were pure fiction. Human nature, I suppose. When hostilities stopped, so did censoring.

Then came the big day. I was on duty in the radio shack in July 1945 when I received the following message in plain language:

THE WAR IS OVER. THE JAPS SURRENDER.

And that was it. So many of us had been through a war and were still not old enough to vote or legally buy a beer. So be it.

Then began the unimaginably difficult task of returning all the troops back to the U.S.A. We finally boarded a troop transport ship on some date in September or early October. A sad thing happened during boarding. When we left New Guinea, we smuggled a dog aboard ship with us that we had adopted. We named her Portside. We brought Portside with us to the dock, where she sat and watched us board. We yelled and waved at her from the top deck. She sat there and whimpered, feeling abandoned. And she was, poor thing.

Once onboard we were informed that our destination was Seattle, Washington. Life aboard this ship was quite a contrast to the conditions aboard the Day Star two years earlier. We were still crowded, but all the ship's facilities were designed for passenger transport. We had cleaning duties, but that was it. And there were movies, or I should say, a movie. I think I saw, "To Have or Have Not" at least seven times. There were a lot of card games going on, which brings me to another sad story.

Just a couple of days out of Seattle we got the call of "Man overboard!" The ship slowed and circled, searching for what seemed like hours. The story on the missing man was that he was a submariner who had been out in the Pacific for five years. He had lost a great deal of his savings aboard this ship and decided to take his own life. He was never found.

When we arrived off the coast of Washington and sailed in through Puget Sound, we were met by a vessel carrying a crowd of people, yelling and screaming their welcome-home to us. It was quite an emotional experience.

I was assigned to a cargo ship that was in dry dock at a port in Bremerton, Washington. While awaiting discharge, we were tasked with duties such as Shore Patrol, hauling in drunks to the brig. As one might imagine, after 2-3 years of wartime discipline, the sudden relative freedom, combined with the ease of obtaining alcohol, well, things could get out of hand. They did, but never anything spectacular. I finally received my discharge in January 1946, three years, nine months and 23 days after I enlisted. Oddly enough, my boyhood friend (Melvin Chrisman) and I arrived back in the neighborhood the same day.

Sansapor Beach Party. The author is fourth from the left, only his head is visible next to the man wearing the helmet.

Author (far right) with three buddies in Subic Bay, Philippines, right after war ended.

Part 3

The Interim Years

Getting used to being out of the controlled military environment took some time. Work was hard to come by. I hadn't finished high school when I left for the Navy, so I took a series of equivalency tests to get my diploma. I tried college for a short period at an extension of the University of Oregon near Portland. That didn't last long. Then I got acquainted with a man who had moved into the house next door while I was away. He was a musician who headed a big band, playing dates mostly in and around Portland. He asked if I would be interested in a job working at the location where he and his band were then playing. I took the job, working behind the soft drink bar. Hard drinks could only be served in specially licensed places, and patrons had to bring their own booze, surrender it to the bartender for mixing, and then buy it back from him. Strange, but accepted at the time. In this job I served sober people instead of drunks.

By far the best part of this job was meeting the love of my life, Barbara Ann Bloch. She was the singer who fronted my neighbor's big band. I had seen her picture at the front entrance and thought, "Wow, what a beauty!" I didn't work there long, but long enough to meet Barbara. We started dating. I was 21 by then and soon discovered she was only 17, working on a special permit. "My God," I thought, "I'm dating a baby!" I'm 93 now, and she's 89. The age difference became meaningless a long time ago.

When we were dating, Barbara lived on the northeast side of Portland, and I lived in southeast. Public transportation was the only way to get together. I finally saved enough to buy a car, a 1935 Ford two-door, making courting a great deal easier. I am sure she will always remember our first date. I took her to a restaurant very near the skid row district. She became increasingly nervous the closer we got to the place. Once we entered the restaurant, she relaxed. It was beautifully appointed, and they had a corner on the local fried oysters market — small delicate morsels fresh from the waters off Olympia, Washington.

One of my best friends from early school days had sailed with the Merchant Marine during the war. He talked me into joining the seaman's union. He and I sailed on one cargo ship together. The captain of the ship was Scandinavian and spoke very broken English. We couldn't understand him. When either of us had the wheel and were given a command, for example, "Come left to 090 degrees and hold steady," we would come back with, "What?" or "Say again." After a few of these exchanges, the skipper would call for a new man on the wheel.

This was a coastal vessel, so when we arrived back to our home port in Portland, we were both summarily fired.

My next trip was as an ordinary seaman aboard a World War II cargo ship called the Council Bluffs Victory. Hundreds of these were built for the war effort, some of which were purchased by private shipping companies. This was a voyage carrying lumber from Coos Bay, Oregon, to ports on the east coast. We took on lumber in each cargo bay and stacked it high on the fore and aft decks. The head seaman aboard this vessel was a very tough guy who put up with no nonsense. That was demonstrated just before we left the dock in Portland. Two of the deck hands were having a brawl in one of the sleeping quarters when he came in and put them both down. That never happened again.

We reached Panama in a few days, then had to wait our turn through the locks. We made use of our time chipping and repainting on the sides of the ship. In transiting the canal, a ship must pass through the Gatun Lake, stop, and wait for the next level to fill. While we were stopped there, we all stripped down and dove off the lumber cargo into the beautiful water below. In the heat of Panama, the cool water of the lake was making our day, until we heard this: "There are sharks in these waters boys." So that took care of that. Vendors could come alongside and climb aboard with their wares during this waiting period. One who came aboard spoke only Japanese. One of our seaman, a white guy from NYC, began dickering with the guy in his native tongue. It blew the vendor away. I'm sure he sold him every-thing at cost. The seaman told us that learning foreign languages was his only hobby.

After we completed our west-to-east passage through the can-al, we traveled on up the east coast to dock at a port in Balti-more. I took a draw from the purser, i.e., I got paid. I walked up the dock to the nearest bar. It was a typical 1940s bar, sawdust on the floor, shuffle board, pool table, and populated by the usual booze parlor crowd. I played shuffle board with the young waitress/bartender in the place and soon nicknamed her Stinky. It was hot, and she didn't bother to shave under her arms. Then some drunk at the bar got on my case for no good reason. I ended up giving him a good right shot to the mouth at the same time he was throwing up his lunch. Big mistake, because this guy was huge, with muscles on his muscles. My shot, unfortunately, just got his attention. I was already on my way back to the ship when I notice this monster coming down the road after me. At the same time, our big, tough head seaman was heading toward us from the ship. He saw the developing situation and told me to keep on going and he'd take care of it. He did, and that was that.

The following day we continued up the coast to New York, docking at Brooklyn. Here is where I considered signing off the ship to look for a berth on one heading for Europe. My brother was still listed as missing in action, and I thought maybe I could learn something about him over there from the Army. While we were docked in Brooklyn, the seaman's union went on strike with the stipulation that ships could return to home ports before crews would strike. That killed my plans for a voyage to Europe. We headed back with a cargo of whiskey, back through the Panama Canal and up the west coast, docking at Long Beach, California, to unload the cargo. When inventory was taken of the off-loaded cargo, only two cases of whiskey were missing, an unusually low number according to veteran seamen. Longshoremen have never been known for their restraint in rewarding themselves for a day's work with a few samples of the vast amounts of goods they handle. So be it.

It was sometime in June of 1946 that my mother received notice of her son Larry's confirmed death. One of the duties of the U.S. Army's occupying force in Europe was to scour all the known combat areas for evidence on missing men. My brother had been found buried in a cemetery somewhere in East Germany. He was later moved and buried in a U.S. military cemetery in Belgium. While I was still in New Guinea I received a V-mail from my brother's commanding officer. He wrote that they had been in a big fight over Berlin that day, March 6, 1944. It was on the way back to England that he had to bail out. His chute was seen to open, but that is the last anyone saw of him. Exactly how he was killed remains a mystery. My mother now had to deal with another loss to this war. I am sure it was these events, plus her breakup with my father, that led her to join the Army herself. She served a short period in the medical branch, stationed at a hospital in Vancouver, Washington.

By now, life was progressing at a slow and uneventful pace, a job here, a job there. So in 1948 I signed up for the fall term at the University of Oregon, financed by the G.I. Bill. That didn't last long. For one thing, the subsistence allowed under the G.I. Bill never came through. I washed dishes in a local restaurant at night to meet expenses. Life would have been completely dull except that Barbara was still singing with the band, and their sessions were broadcast over the radio most nights. I would tune her in and forget the books. Also, at that time I was becoming very interested in flying. Since my brother had been a fighter pilot, I suppose that's what I really wanted to be. One thing tipped the scales on my decision. The Air force was now accepting married men, age 21 to 25, into the Aviation Cadet program. I went back to Portland, got a steady job working for a steel company, and in January 1949, Barbara and I were married. In the meantime, I had taken and passed all the exams required for the Cadet program and was then put on a waiting list for the next opening.

The notice to report for duty came in the spring of 1949. I boarded a train, leaving Barbara pregnant with our first child, Michelle, and left for a base located near San Angelo, Texas, called Goodfellow Field. I was assigned rail transportation, the destination being San Angelo, Texas. My father met me at the station to see me off. Just before departure time he handed me a paper sack with a pint of whiskey enclosed. I think it was Four Roses or some such popular brand of the time. I had Pullman privileges, and assigned an upper bunk. As the day progressed into night the crew began preparing the Pullmans for night duty. I noticed a young Asian girl cuddling her obviously very new baby. She didn't have a sleeper. Since I was nervous about taking on my new life style and having by then consumed about half of that pint of whiskey, I was convinced I wouldn't be sleeping that night. I offered the girl and her baby my bunk for her seat. She accepted.

She put the baby in first, but being quite short, she required help getting up and into the bunk herself. The only part available for me to push was her rear end, which I proceeded to use with no audible objections from her. Just then the conductor appeared. First impressions are never reliable for final decisions. Thinking I was taking advantage of this girl, the conductor lost it. I couldn't convince him, and he got nastier. I gave him a quick left to the nose followed by a right cross to the side of his head. He went down. After a bit he got up and headed for the next car ahead, screaming all sorts of vitriol in my direction. So I followed him in between cars and dropped him again. When he got up this time he decided not to open his big mouth.

When I finally arrived at San Angelo I was met and transported to Goodfellow Field. After settling in, I was taken to an area for indoctrination into the program. I was escorted to a private room. A gentleman walked in, sat down across from me and said, "If you hadn't gotten this far you would already be out of the program." He then proceeded to read a telegram they had received from some office of the railroad explaining their version of how the incident went down, accusing me of attempting to molest the young mother. After I explained the real circumstances to this gentleman, he settled down and continued with my introduction and indoctrination.

Goodfellow had World War II-style barracks and dirt runways. Most cadets were three to four years younger than I, and recent college graduates. I remember one exceptionally bright cadet from Annapolis, Maryland, who helped me with math problems in our ground school sessions. He later washed out of the flying program, as did many others. Having wartime experience, I was already aware of the necessity for strict discipline. The ones new to the military were not, and discipline was the name of the game in every activity, even eating: back straight, eyes straight ahead, food brought from plate to the mouth in a square manner, chew and repeat. It took some getting used to. Then there was the demerit system. For every so many demerits you walked so many tours on the parade ground with a rifle on your shoulder. This didn't happen to me until after our first break from the routine. We were finally allowed to make a visit to the town of San Angelo. Sure enough, I got into a fight with one of the locals. This one, as I recall, I won decisively, which is probably why it was reported to the authorities on the base. The following day the base commander sent word for me to report to him in his office. He said, "Sit down, and let's have a talk." It turned out that he had been one of the pilots who flew a B-25 off the deck of the aircraft carrier Hornet to perform that famous raid on Tokyo early in the war. We spent the better part of an hour exchanging war stories. I learned I had been turned in by another cadet. Just before I left the commander's office he said, "Don't worry about that jerk who turned you in. I'll take care of him." I did walk tours on the parade ground just to make everything look kosher.

The T-6 Texan is not an easy aircraft to fly, and especially tricky to land. The saying goes: There are those who have ground-looped a T-6 on landing, and those who will. There was no runway laid out in a nice concrete strip at Goodfellow. It was just a big, square, dirt field. We practiced our landings into the wind, whichever direction that might be. The winds in West Texas can get strong and unpredictable. Sometimes, we would get caught with dozens of airplanes in the air when one of those big blows would come up. Fortunately, we always managed to get them all down safely, probably because, by then, the weak cadets had washed out.

Training was going along fine, but what about the home front? Then it came, the telegram I had been waiting for. The baby had arrived, a healthy bundle of joy. Michelle Ann Ferguson made her first appearance on August 4, 1949. Barbara had managed the process nicely in Portland. That is to say, I didn't hear the screams in Texas.

Those of us chosen for fighter training were sent either to Las Vegas, Nevada, for conventional training in the P-51 Mustang, or to Chandler, Arizona, for jet training in the F-80. I was sent to Williams, where my brother Larry completed advanced training in 1943. While we were learning the intricacies of the jet engine — its properties, thrust to weight ratios, etc. — we would stay current in the air by continuing to fly the T-6. Michelle is now six months old. Barbara is 20. So, she packs up clothes, baby bottles, and a load of diapers, and boards a train for Phoenix. Pampers haven't come on the market yet, and these cloth diapers have to be washed on the move. Somehow she made it, and we found a one-room converted garage apartment in Mesa, Arizona. It had a kitchen/bedroom area with a foldout bed and a toilet/shower bathroom. It was all we could afford, and I could be there only on the weekends. Occasionally, I would fly over the apartment in a T-6 and do a slow roll to let her know I was thinking of her. It wasn't easy for her with the new baby. For example, she had to pack up the dirty clothes, get the baby ready, and board a bus to get to the nearest laundromat, then repeat the routine for return to the apartment. It was 1950. Caring for Michelle was her only "entertainment" during the week. There was no television.

F-80 training finally began in earnest. A two-seated aircraft had been developed for training called the T-33. The instructor occupied the rear seat with intercom to the student in the front. It turned out that I was the first in our class to solo the single-seated F-80A. This is how it worked out. A weekend cross-country navigation mission had been scheduled. I was allowed to remain at the base because Barbara and Michelle were there. The group departed early Friday. After they were gone, my instructor came up to me and asked, "Do you think you're ready?" Naturally I said "Yes, Sir." Even now, with thousands of hours of flying time behind me in all kinds of jet fighters under so many different circumstances, I still remember the thrill of that first solo jet flight. After graduation I was assigned to the 78th Fighter Group stationed at Hamilton Field just north of San Francisco, in Marin County, California. Barbara and I went into debt to buy a 1948 Chevrolet convertible, and we headed north for our first assignment.

Hamilton Field was one of the best geographical assignments in the continental U.S. However, the fighter group here was equipped with the oldest jet fighters in the inventory, the F-84D. Four of us from the class at Williams were assigned here. One was killed in a gunnery training flight over the ocean not long after we arrived. A wing separated from his aircraft as he pulled off the target. We knew we had chosen a dangerous profession and would be expected to continue on after such incidents. And so we did. I flew again that afternoon. Over the course of our assignment there, many more accidents would occur. Also, not long after our arrival there my father died of a heart attack. He had been in and out of the Veteran's hospital in Portland for some time, so it wasn't a surprise. Thanks to the speed of the T-33, I was able to fly up there and see him just before he passed.

One flight experience as a newly ordained fighter pilot a few months after arriving at Hamilton Field went like this: I was assigned lead pilot for a cross country navigation training flight, with a really new guy on my wing. We departed late one afternoon and landed at Moses Lake, Washington. That night we took off for some required night formation training. The night sky was clear but moonless. I filed for a local area VFR flight clearance. (Yes, it was legal then.) After takeoff and climb to altitude, I made the brilliant decision to expand the local area to include my home town, Portland, Oregon. As we slowly descended from altitude, I located the neighborhood and the house my mother still lived in. With my wingman tucked in tight, I set us up for a low, high-speed pass above the house. To do it, we had to fly over not only other neighborhoods, but also over a park where softball games and other activities were being enjoyed. I should point out that jet aircraft were rarely seen or heard in this area at that time. It was the Cold War era, the Korean conflict was in its early stages, and the general population wasn't sure what might come next. Hearing this sudden, loud, and unfamiliar sound created a reaction you might expect. Panic.

When we landed back at Moses Lake we were met by all sorts of officials. There was no way out for us. It seems we were flying the only two jets in the area that night. The local Portland newspaper hit us hard with editorial articles accompanied by a nasty cartoon of a woman waving a broom at an overhead jet. After we flew back to Hamilton, the investigation began. One of the experienced pilots from another squadron in our fighter group was assigned to lead the investigation. He interviewed many individuals who had witnessed the event, to include the commander of the National Guard Fighter Group stationed at Portland International Airport. He made the following state-ment, "Several of my pilots witnessed the event and all claimed these pilots were at or well above the minimum required altitude of one thousand feet." What else would one expect from another fighter pilot? To further complicate matters, the pilot assigned to investigate my incident became involved in his own. On one bright, Sunday afternoon in San Francisco, he flew an F-84 at very low altitude across Kezar Stadium while the San Francisco 49er football game was in play. This meant we now had an inves-tigator investigating the investigator. The bad Portland Journal news about my incident continued until my old boyhood bud-dy's father wrote to them in no uncertain terms (with good back-up) to kindly knock it off. They did, and the whole event faded into history.

Marin County was a great area to live and raise children, and it wasn't long before our next baby was due. Larry Newton Ferguson was born December 18, 1950. We named him after my brother. The Korean War had already begun. I had volunteered to go with the first 20 replacements in fighter squadrons already there. This is when I first heard about the Sullivan Law. During World War II in the Pacific Theater, five brothers were assigned together aboard one tactical fighting ship. They were all killed when the ship took heavy losses during an engagement with Japanese fighting vessels. The Sullivan family lost all their sons. Congress then passed a law stating that, in addition to prohibiting family members from serving together in the same combat unit, sole surviving sons could not serve in combat areas. Since I was the sole surviving son in my family, headquarters applied this law and kept me in place. Of the first group of pilots from our squadron to go to Korea as replacements, we lost almost 50 percent. I guess I was fortunate to be held back awhile, although the saying in the fighter business is, "go to war early before the ground gunners get so much practice."

In 1952 I was chosen to attend a career-broadening course in Montgomery, Alabama called Squadron Officers School. We stored most of our belongings, packed our bags into our now newer car, a 1950 Mercury two-door, and headed south with two babies and no air conditioning. In those days, neither shoulder straps nor child seats were required or even invented. Barbara had little trouble in turning around and whacking an unruly kid or two. We stayed there for about two months, learning a lot about their culture and their legal system. The first thing we noticed was separate everything for whites and blacks. As for their court system, I got a firsthand look. I had participated in an afterclass ballgame at the base. When the game was over, we all stopped at the Officers' club for a drink. I had one and left. On the way home, I turned a corner that had gravel scattered on top of the concrete and skidded. A cop in a nearby car saw that and stopped me, smelled my breath, and cited me for driving under the influence. I took a blood test, which proved I was well within the sobriety range. The duty judge charged me anyway and proudly announced, "That fine will be a hunded dollahs, and foh dollahs cote costs." So much for Southern justice. We left there in July in the suffocating heat and humidity. It was a tough drive with no air conditioning, but being young, we looked forward to each day as a new adventure.

*Scotty and Barbara at graduation day for advance pilot train-
ing at Williams Air Force Base in Chandler, Arizona.*

SKETCHES OF AN EARLIER TIME

Barbara sings with a Portland big band in 1946, when Scotty first met his future wife.

Part 4

The Korean War

That same year the squadron was relocated to Paine Field near Everett, Washington. We found a house to rent in a very rural area of Everett where a family of bears never allowed our garbage cans to remain upright. We had changed aircraft to the F-89, a twin-engine interceptor. We weren't there long when I received orders for Korea. I had time to get the family situated in Portland, near Barbara's parents. We found an apartment large enough for her and the two kids, but now she was pregnant with our third child. She surveyed the situation and declared it would work, with one condition: she insisted on a TV. So, we went into debt for a 17-inch black-and-white. I left in December of 1952 aboard ship out of San Francisco, again. This time I am an officer and got better quarters than the last time I sailed under that gate. I wondered why I was traveling by ship, which takes nearly two weeks, when I could fly over in a couple of days. I would soon find out.

When I arrived in Japan, my orders were to join a F-94 interceptor squadron. Apparently, the Sullivan Law didn't apply to this assignment. I wanted nothing to do with that, so I started lobbying for a combat assignment in Korea. One of the assignment guys took pity and got orders issued for me to report to 5th Air Force rear, located at Taegu. 5th Air Force forward was located in Seoul, which I would visit some time later. My preference was to fly with one of the F-86 squadrons located north of there. He had my Form 5 in front of him, which is a log of my flying experience. He asked in which aircraft I was now current. I told him truthfully that it was the F-86. Prior to shipping out, I had stopped by Hamilton AFB and gotten a quick check-out in the F-86F model, flying two flights for a total of two hours and fifteen minutes. He saw this, and then looked at my F-84 time, which was over 500 hours. The F-84 wing was right across the field from this office. He said, "I can assign you to an F-86 group, but you probably won't get more than eight missions a month. If you fly '84s, you will fly all the missions you want. Your choice." I chose the F-84. This turned out to be the new F-84G model with a completely new and beefed-up airframe. It also had a newer, better cockpit design than the D model I had flown, with the throttle at a right angle like an F-51D Mustang. I felt really comfortable in it immediately. Sometime before my arrival, the group was flying the F-84D-11, which was an old D airframe equipped with a higher performance engine. During a group-effort mission against the bridges at Sinanju, the group lost eight pilots and eight airplanes due to a wing coming off during the pullout from their dive-bomb run. The flak there was always heavy, but these losses were attributed to wing failure. As a result, all D models were immediately grounded and replaced with the completely redesigned G.

When I reported for duty to the 58th Fighter Group, I was assigned to the 310th Fighter Squadron. Since there were no openings – each pilot did 100 missions, or one year – I did my flying in the T-33. I took many of the crew chiefs up along the 38th parallel, especially at night, so they could observe all the artillery fire going back and forth. I thought this would give them a better understanding and feel for what they were contributing to back at the home base. Besides, they loved every minute of it. The base was laid out like this: the control tower was on the opposite side of the field, and a little farther on was the city of Taegu. The runway was concrete, but all taxiways were pierced steel planking (PSP). The quarters and out-buildings were shack-like with a dirty stucco on the outer walls. There was a central community shower with cold water only. We had a central mess hall, a makeshift Officers' Club, and an Enlisted Club. Latrines were outhouses within the base and along the flight line, serviced by smallish Korean men with funny hats. They would collect the excrement with what was known in the trade as honey buckets. They used the content of the honey buckets to fertilize their crops. Because of this, I never drove off the base. The smell was overpowering.

When I first started flying combat missions in Korea, I was strictly a wingman or, green sixteen, the position assigned to the newest pilot in any formation of fighters. Due to a pilot rotation opening, I had previously been transferred to another unit — the 69th Fighter Squadron. My first mission was a laugher, taking out a very tall smoke stack out on the Haeju Peninsula, just north of the 38th parallel. It was undefended, but no one had brought it down in the almost three years of the war. In another early mission, I'm in trail on the lead pilot as we descend on what appeared to be several rural houses. He began laying down some heavy strafing. I never touched my gun switch because I saw clothes hanging on lines behind the houses. In his defense, we were all told that anything north of the parallel was fair game. On another occasion, we were on a napalm run against housing for a troop concentration. I'm in trail position on the lead pilot when I see him unload two cans of napalm on one running soldier. This was not only overkill to me, but quite disgusting. And there was the time coming off a bombing mission in a heavily defended area near the Chinese border. I was exiting the area, staying low, and as I descended over a hill I saw dozens of people running in all directions. I went for the gun switch but didn't fire when I saw the people were dressed in bright-colored clothes, not uniforms. What action was taken by the following fighters, I never wanted to know. I didn't dwell on such incidents. The combatants north of the parallel had a lot to answer for, also.

From then on, the missions got more hazardous for me. The North Koreans had flak traps everywhere. For example, in one area there was a railroad tunnel entrance which looked so inviting for a strike. But just start rolling in on it and you quickly disturbed a hornet's nest of 37mm anti-aircraft guns. You needed to learn quickly where the bad spots were. Many of our missions were far north, near the Chinese border. On several missions that required an entire squadron or more, we would be escorted to the target by high-flying F-86 fighters. When the MiG-15s out of Antung, China, came across the border to intercept us, the F-86s above us would jettison their external fuel tanks to lighten up for the fight. When this happened, all that metal would come floating down through our formations. I don't recall anyone ever being hit, but what were the odds?

We flew all types of missions with all manner of purpose. Night intruder missions consisted of one airplane, one pilot, two 500-pound bombs, and 1800 50-caliber machine gun rounds. The F-84G had six guns, two in the nose section and two in each wing. On these night missions we would fly lights out along the North Korean main supply routes. When we would spot truck traffic lights moving south, which we almost always did, we would cut the throttle back to reduce the noise factor, drop the nose into a shallow dive and release the bombs. But they had guns, too, and they always fired back. My favorite night mission was near the town of Sinanju. Several times before, when I had flown over this area on a night mission, they had spotted me with their radar-controlled lights, followed by AA blasts. This night my target was up near the Russian border. On the way out, I purposely flew over the same area and, sure enough, here come the lights. When I got directly over them, I rolled over, pulled the nose through into a tight spiral dive, closed my eyes and squeezed the trigger down, sending 50-calibers from six guns right down their chute. The lights below went out. Six guns firing directly in front of you on a black night will destroy your night vision, big time. Hence, the momentary closing of the eyes. This move was both stupid, and effective.

On my worst mission, we were near Sinanju with a huge gaggle, skip-bombing into a mud dam. On a target like this, I always strafed the area on my way in. This time, when I pressed the gun switch, two rounds came out and that was it. Climbing out away from the target area, two MiG-15 fighters passed just in front of me. All I had to do was bank slightly right, pull up on their tale and they're toast. With nothing to fight with, I had to go full throttle and pull up into the cloud cover above to survive. Nightmare stuff. After landing, I discovered that this airplane had flown an intruder mission the previous night and had fired out. The armament crews missed that one and it cost me.

On my best mission, I had a flight of four doing behind-the-lines reconnaissance. A forward air controller flying a T-6 called for help for some Marines who were under heavy fire at the base of a mountain. When we got into these situations, we were required to ask for authentication, which I did. The FAC came back with, "We don't have time for that, and besides, I have too many holes in this bird now to wait any longer." When we got in position, he called for me to hit his smoke. I put two 500-pound bombs in there, followed by six more of the same from the other three F-84s. When the smoke cleared, he called out in some very colorful language that not only had we taken out the bad guys, but that the whole mountainside was caving in. Our headquarters later received a very appreciative letter from the Marine officer in command of that unit. I slept well that night.

A different kind of positive experience occurred when the squadron was returning from a long-distance mission with every aircraft low on fuel. We heard a panic call come over the squadron frequency: "Help me, somebody! Will someone please help me?" I called him and got him onto our emergency frequency, and squared him away on his heading, altitude, and state of fuel. Shortly afterwards, his engine flamed out. By then I'm in the traffic pattern and ready to land. There were heavy clouds with occasional breaks in the overcast that day. I told him to glide to 10, 000 feet and if he didn't have a good view of the field for a dead-stick landing, punch out. As I was taxiing in, he called at 10,000 feet with no visibility. I quickly went through the ejection procedures with him and he was out of there. After I pulled into the parking area, I told my crew chief to look for a parachute, as I knew it had to be nearby. Sure enough, here comes an F-84 flying straight and level about 1,000 feet above the control tower, silent, with no canopy. It then veered off to the right, nose down, and crashed. Out of the overcast a few seconds later appears the pilot in his parachute, touching down just at the edge of the field, unhurt.

Of course, there were sad times. As the assistant operations officer, I scheduled the combat missions. One day during quite a push up north, our headquarters was calling for all sorts of ordinance for various targets. Napalm missions were the most dangerous because of the low altitude, hold-it-steady type delivery. One pilot had already flown two napalm sorties, so I switched with him for the third napalm run, scheduling him for the relatively safe, behind-the-lines recce mission. It didn't turn out that way. I came back. He didn't. He ran into an unknown, heavily defended area and took a hit directly in the canopy. That was, hands-down, my worst day there.

I still have a Zippo cigarette lighter that I acquired while I was in Korea. I say acquired because I never paid for it. Here's the story. During a mission in a heavy flak area, one of our pilots took a hit that shattered his canopy, sending minute particles of the plastic canopy into both eyes, literally blinding him. The flight lead got on his wing and found he could still communicate; so, he became the wounded man's eyes, giving him commands for small movements of the flight controls, both stick and throttle. They flew like this to a forward F-86 base designated K-14. When they reached the landing pattern altitude, things would really get tricky. Now, it would be gear-down time, flaps, and small stick and throttle adjustments. The blinded pilot was having nothing to do with that. His wingman stayed with him down to just before the blinded pilot cut the throttle to the off position. He touched down, gear up. As he was sliding down the runway, he sensed that he was on fire, so he reached down and pulled the ejection handles. In those days we didn't have zero-altitude ejection capability. He just figured that was his only alternative to burning to death. This next part was described to me later by an eyewitness. During the ejection, he ascended, doing a couple of rotations, and then descended, landing upside-down with the corner of the ejection seat absorbing most of the shock. His only wound was a broken collarbone. He was then transported to a U.S. hospital in Japan. While he was there, we contacted him to order us cigarette lighters with the squadron insignia implanted, which he did, but had no money to pay for them. His nurse, being gracious as most nurses are, loaned him the money. I don't know whether the nurse was ever repaid, but we got our Zippos, thanks to her. We later heard that he regained his sight but would probably never fly again.

On another day we had a pilot take a hit in one of his wing-tip fuel tanks, engulfing it in flames. At the time, the closest base was K-14. He called their tower for an emergency landing. On the rollout, the tank was still on fire when he asked, "Where do you want me to park this thing?" This guy was some cool customer. I went up to that base later to bring our now repaired airplane back home. After taxiing out to the holding area for takeoff, I was told to hold for an aerial demonstration. It was quite good and entertaining, but I was in no mood for that nonsense right then. I later found out that the pilot of the F-86 doing the demonstration was a civilian test pilot for North American Aviation Corp. named Bob Hoover, probably the most famous test pilot back then. I would bet that he got in a few combat missions while he was there. Charles Lindberg did the same thing with the P-38 in the Pacific theater during World War II.

We had a rather complicated instrument approach procedure at K-2. It involved the use of two radio beacons. As you passed over one and started your descent, you had to look away from your instruments to tune in the second station, invariably causing severe vertigo. Once you became accustomed to the procedure there was no problem. One day I was up on a test hop for a minor maintenance problem, flying under a heavy overcast. A marine pilot, flying an F-9 single-seated fighter, called the tower and asked them to read him the letdown procedures. He said he was on top of the overcast. I broke in and told him where I was and what I was flying, and that I would climb up and bring him in on my wing. He declined the offer, saying he could handle it. He didn't, and it cost him his life.

My last big mission occurred shortly before the ceasefire was declared. The mission was to break the dam above Pyongyang, which was their fresh water supply. We referred to the North Korean Capital as Ping Pong. This would involve the entire wing of F-84s. We would be loaded with two 750-pound bombs and 1800 rounds of 50-caliber ammunition each. It was summer, so it would require JATO (jet assisted takeoff.) The runway was long enough, but there was a hill several hundred feet above runway elevation affectionately called "Bust your ass hill." With this load, we needed the extra push to make it over that hill. We would punch off the JATO containers immediately after burnout.

A lot of planning went into this mission, and it completed successfully. We broke the dam, which I am convinced helped precipitate the agreement for a permanent ceasefire. Our return to K-2 was very interesting. A big, beautiful Constellation transport aircraft, carrying the Army Chief of Staff, General J. Laughton Collins, had just landed. It was taxiing back down the runway even though the control tower operator had directed the pilot to taxi back to the parking ramp on the PSP taxiways. The pilot replied that he didn't want that crap (referring to the mud under the PSP) on this airplane. The first fighter pilot, who was just about to break into his overhead pattern, hit his mike and said, "You'd better get that big son of a bitch off the runway. We've got 48 fighters, all low on fuel, coming in for landing." The big Connie took the next exit off the runway and sat there until the last F-84 had taxied in.

Sometime before the big raid on the dam, two of us were given the opportunity to spend a little time with Army grunts on the front lines. We first stopped at Seoul, enormous today, but not much of a city at the time. It had been overrun by North Korean forces on their march south to Pusan at the southern tip of Korea, and then again when the allied forces pushed them back north of the 38th Parallel. We were transported by Jeep to our respective assigned units at a base camp near the foot of a mountain nicknamed Papasan. I had laid down a few bombs there in the past. The fight against the North Korea forces was being carried out by multinational forces, including those from Greece. My companion from our fighter group happened to be of Greek origin, so they put him with a Greek detachment. I went with an American artillery unit. While there, I got a close-in look at an air strike by U.S. Navy Corsair fighters in support of an infantry engagement. My escorts pointed out to me how much stuff the enemy threw at us during one of these strikes. One soldier said, "Hell, they even throw rocks." My companion told me on the way out that the Greek fighters were something else. They would crawl out on moonless nights armed only with knives and create all sorts of hell for the enemy. Just like our night intruder flights, I thought, only somewhat more up-close and personal.

On July 27, 1953 an armistice was signed, ending three years and one month of some intense fighting. However, we weren't quite finished. What the general population probably never knew was the caveat that applied to each side: we could still shoot at each other for 12 more hours. And we did. The North Koreans must have gotten a heads-up on this, because on that last day we encountered unusually heavy flak all along the parallel. I flew three missions that day. We all did. The gun barrels on my 50-calibers got so hot on my third mission, the ammo started cooking off after I released the gun switch. Scary stuff because I thought I was taking hits.

The next day was strange to say the least. The non-stop action on the flight line was missing. There was a temporary halt in operations all around. Wartime action to peacetime training had to be thought out and coordinated. The first thing our squadron came up with was to do a full-blown fly-by in salute to all the maintenance personnel who had kept our fighters in such good shape throughout our time there. I was assigned the privilege of planning and leading the formation. It was reported beautifully performed, and not a shot was fired at us. That took some getting used to, flying anywhere without someone on the ground contesting your presence.

Part of the peacetime changes included arrival of new pilots who required training and indoctrination to area operations. We opened an old gunnery range located several miles north of K-2, adjacent to the Naktong River. The river curved at that spot, leaving a long sandy beach area. One day I was on duty there in the control tower, directing several flights of F-84s making strafing runs on targets we had placed on the beach. One of the pilots in the firing pattern called in, saying his engine had flamed out and that he couldn't restart. I advised him to eject immediately if he had the altitude. He replied that he did, but he would rather dead-stick it in and land on the beach, gear up. As he passed by the tower I could see fire coming out of his speed brake area. When he touched down on the edge of the beach, the engine exploded, scattering pieces of his aircraft far ahead. I had already run out of the tower and started swimming across the river to reach the crash area. When I got there, I found the pilot still strapped into his ejection seat and on fire. Each time I attempted to release his shoulder harness and lap belt, flames would flare up. I kept throwing sand on him to get the fire out. Once I had his body separated from the seat, it could be removed from the area. A Marine helicopter came in to do just that. It was a hot summer day, and the inside of the helicopter was even hotter. I suddenly realized I was being watched by two local men or older boys. They must have witnessed the entire event. Each time I tried to release the pilot from the seat and the flames would flare up, these two would giggle as if it was the funniest thing they had ever seen. We knew we had enemies scattered among the locals. For example, one time when the ground crews went to the flight line early in the morning to prep our airplanes for that day's mission, they found the pitot tubes on every plane bent in half. That meant we would have no static instrument operation, which meant we were all grounded that day. Thank goodness I had left my sidearm in the control tower or we might very well have had an international incident. I was really pissed. The swim back across the Naktong helped cool my senses as well as my body. Headquarters then advised us to remove the electronic identification equipment, if possible, and continue flying operations. They would send in a crew the following day to remove the wreckage. The next day I had to tell them, "Forget it. There's nothing left." Overnight, the locals had scavenged every piece of the wreckage, leaving only a black mark across the sand. It remains a mystery to me how they managed to cart off some of the heavier pieces, like the engine, so fast.

I had completed 85 combat missions. Those with closer to 100 missions, like over 90, were reassigned back to the States. I spent the remainder of my time as a test pilot at Fukuoka, Japan, where our rear-echelon maintenance was done. While there, three of us took a taxi into town. The driver said he didn't speak

English. The two guys with me were talking about how wonderful they thought the Japanese people were. I broke in, saying "I wouldn't trust one of these little bastards any farther than I could throw him across the street." The driver's reaction was immediate. He understood English, alright. Things have changed so much since then, but I still harbored some animosity toward the Japanese in those days, left in me from World War II. However, I do remember getting a great haircut and a neck-and-shoulder massage from a female barber while there. My barber back at Taegu had such bad breath from eating buried, rotten kimchee that I insisted he chew on some breath neutralizer long enough to kill the stink before I would let him get close enough to cut my hair.

There was a special moment near the end of my short tour at Fukuoka. One morning I was out on the ramp, waiting for my F-84 to be brought out from the hanger for test. It was just about sun-up when I looked toward the seaward end of the runway. Coming in about 50 feet off the Strait of Korea and heading directly for our runway was an F-86, trailed by a ball of vapor. As he passed over the far end of the runway, the pilot pulled the aircraft up and out of the vapor into a vertical climb, rolling so fast you couldn't count the number. My eyes watered with emotion. It's a fighter pilot thing.

For all the flying, fighting, casualties, camaraderie, and yes, excitement, the most important thing that happened to me during my time over there was the birth of our third child and second daughter, Renee Marie, on March 8, 1953. Barbara wrote that she was managing with the apartment she had. It was just one bedroom, but large. She managed to fit a full-size bed, two twin beds, and a baby crib in there, with room to spare. I imagine she got even less sleep each night than I did. She had adapted to the military lifestyle quite nicely, writing that she had washed the car the day before Renee was born. That girl had, and still has, true grit.

I left Fukuoka aboard a C-54 transport for San Francisco, sometime in October 1953. I don't know how it got started, but during the first year of the Korean war, a fighter pilot left a full bottle of whiskey with a bartender at the bar at the top of the Mark Hopkins Hotel (fondly known as The Top of the Mark), with instructions to give it to the next Korean combat fighter pilot that came to the bar. That pilot would in turn replenish the supply before he left, and so on. Two of us, who had returned on the same airplane, went there as our first stop home. Armed with the necessary ingredient, we walked up to the bartender and said, "We're from the 58th Fighter Group, Korea." Sure enough, even though the war was over, the custom was still honored. The bartender stepped over to a special place, pulled out a bottle, brought it to us and said, "Welcome back." We replenished the supply when we left. The next day I caught a commercial airliner for Portland, Oregon. I hadn't seen Barbara, Michelle, or Larry for almost a year, and I had never seen Renee. The reunion was as good as I imagined it would be.

The author exiting from an F-84 in Korea after a test flight.

*The author's picture of his mates
departing for a mission from K-2.*

Taxiing out in the F-84 from K-2
loaded with two 750-lb. bombs.

SKETCHES OF AN EARLIER TIME

The author in front of squadron operations at K-2.

Author in the cockpit: Mission accomplished!

Part 5

The Cold War

After a short vacation, we moved back to the same area of Washington we had left. I was assigned to the same squadron at Paine Field that I left the year before. Most of the faces had changed, and the squadron was now flying the F-86D, designed strictly for shooting down conventionally-powered bombers. It was equipped with air-to-air rockets only. They were carried in a pod, mid-fuselage, which would extend, fire, and retract. The Cold War, in full swing at the time, created widespread hysteria within the military industrial complex that seemed to exploit every idea someone in the top brass threw on the table. The airplane was a pleasure to fly, but the mission for which it was designed ceased to be relevant before it got to the flight line.

We moved into a different kind of neighborhood this time; no bears visiting our back yard. Michelle started first grade and immediately became the boss of her little brother, Larry. Larry was memorialized on many cameras at a church, picking his nose while performing in a play called, "Sailing away with Jesus." Renee was still in swaddling clothes, just being cute. Barbara became the president of the Officers' Wives Club on the first ballot and has been a political junkie ever since.

We were stationed at Paine Field from late 1953 through mid-1955. A few things stand out from that assignment. We were on alert a lot. If our ground radar surveillance station detected any unidentified aircraft heading inbound to our area, we were required to be airborne within five minutes, climb to altitude, identify it by number and type, and stay with it until declared friendly. It was quite a little game we played during that Cold War period. Our ground radar control station was located near Blaine, Washington, which was several miles north of Paine Field. After the mission was completed and the weather permitted, we would drop down to low altitude and buzz the station as a salute to them for good work. One day the squadron got a letter that read like this: "My young son loves to watch your airplanes fly over our house, so please don't stop. But would you please fly a little higher. He has a metal plate in his head, and the vibration from the noise makes his head ache." We established a mandatory minimum altitude from then on.

Another day the squadron received a call from the office of U.S. Senator Henry "Scoop" Jackson. He was to give the eulogy in the city of Spokane for the recently deceased governor of Washington, and he needed to get there fast. I got the assignment to fly him in a T-33. We briefed him on the ejection procedures, the general layout of the cockpit, and for him to keep his hands off everything. This would be his first flight in a jet-powered aircraft of any kind. We took off and climbed just high enough to comfortably clear the mountains, then gently descended toward the landing runway at Geiger Field. Fortunately, I had handed him a burp bag before takeoff. He used it on the rollout several times. I taxied in slowly so he could clean up before facing the crowd awaiting him. It was a different story on the way back. He was now a gung-ho fighter pilot ready for anything. He asked me to fly over his alma-mater, the University of Washington. I thought, "What the hell, he's a U.S. Senator. Why not." So I did, and he loved it. When we arrived back over Paine Field, I asked, "Do you think we should let them know we're back, Senator?" He replied with a definite "Yes!" I made a low, fast pass down the runway, pulled up into a vertical climb, rolled out on top, did a split S followed by a few vertical rolls down. Then we entered the traffic pattern, where I pulled about 4Gs in the break and landed. He was beside himself and couldn't stop talking. There would be no more burp bags for him. He later made two unsuccessful runs to become the Democrat Party's nominee for President of the United States.

Living in the far Northwest almost always involves weather. During one of our summers at Paine Field, the temperature never rose above 68 degrees, which meant the skies were overcast most of the time. I would see the sun on most days, flying above the cloud layers, while Barbara and the kids were stuck down below this dismal goo. Then sometime in early 1955 I received orders to join a newly formed unit designated Tactical Evaluation. We would test the ability of fighter squadrons located in the western U.S. to perform their mission. Once again, we packed up and moved back to Hamilton Field, California, where the sun would greet us most mornings. We rented a three-bedroom house in the small town of Novato. The rent was $110 per month. This sounds low, until you consider my monthly pay was then only $410, and that was with flight pay. Living in this area left us with some of our most indelible and precious memories, the highlight being the birth of our fourth child, Scott Brian, on January 17, 1957. More about that later. Because I would be gone a lot in this job, I needed to make life easier for Barbara in my absence. So we went into debt again and bought a portable dishwasher. The backyard had plenty of room for the kids to play and the house was in a cul-de-sac, so vehicle traffic was little worry. We watched the kids grow and develop all sorts of skills in this short but memorable time.

I had one unsolicited perk in this assignment. We were equipped with two F-86D aircraft. Since I was the only member of the unit qualified to fly them, this was my transportation to and from any F-86D squadron. It also served as the chase airplane I used to evaluate their individual flying abilities. While these airplanes were on the ramp at Hamilton, the assigned crew chiefs would keep them perfectly maintained and shined as if they had just been delivered from the factory. They stood out on the ramp, separated from the local squadron's planes like two sore thumbs, which elicited continual complaints from the squadron commander. It was during one of these trips evaluating a squadron in Washington State that I received a frantic call from Hamilton saying, "Get back here now, your wife is about to have the baby." Having my own airplane available really paid off. I strapped into that cockpit, took off and flew just under Mach 1 all the way back, landing with minimum fuel and making it to the hospital on base just before Scott Brian made his first landing on this planet.

I remained in this small tactical evaluation unit until early 1959. The local squadron had just switched over to the newest fighter in the inventory, the F-104A, the first in the Air Force to do so. It was designed by Kelly Johnson, an aeronautical engineer at the Lockheed Company. He had previously designed the P-38 and the famous U-2 spy plane. The 104 was powered by a General Electric engine with a four-stage afterburner. At altitude, it could reach Mach 2 with very little strain. I had to fly it. I arranged to switch jobs with a pilot in the fighter group's operations department. That airplane was all I thought it would be, and more. It was called, "The missile with the man in it." I found out why on my first flight. You could get to 40, 000 feet fast, and the real estate goes by quickly when you're moving at Mach 2.

As thrilling as it was to fly, we also had some wrecks with the 104, three that I recall. While in a weather let-down, we thought one pilot misread his altimeter from the radio fix on the Farallon Islands and crashed shortly after making landfall. It took several days of search before we found the body. Another pilot lost engine oil pressure during takeoff, aborted too late, and went off the runway into mud flats. He hurt his back but survived. In the beginning, the F-104 was equipped with a downward ejection. We had one pilot use it when his engine quit at 1500 feet. He was one of the few to eject in this system and make it out alive. It was later modified to the standard upward ejection.

The F-104 was the last of so many models of fighters I had flown out of this airfield, including the World War II P-51D Mustang that we flew mostly for towing targets for air-to-air gunnery. We would deploy to Yuma, Arizona for that. It would get so hot in Yuma that before starting the engine on the Mustang, we would wait for the crews to arrange the fabric target hooked to several hundred feet of cable lying on the runway. Otherwise, the engine coolant would overheat and boil over while we waited for the hookup. I also towed targets at Nellis AFB near Las Vegas for an R&D unit that was testing gunsights. Our group commander taught me how to yank rags off the runway to minimize damage to the target. The technique required a very steep climb at near-stall airspeed, literally hanging on the propeller until the target is airborne before assuming a normal climb attitude and speed. This reduced the amount of time the target would drag on the runway. There happened to be a National Guard P-51 squadron deployed there for gunnery training at the same time. One day one of their pilots, taking off with a target, stalled and crashed back on the runway. He wrecked the airplane but wasn't hurt. I heard later that he was just trying to duplicate the way I'd been doing it. I would have told him that I had been taught by the best, a former Eagle Squadron pilot from The Battle of Britain fame -- our Group commander.

We left there in October 1959. This time we were headed for Fairbanks, Alaska. I had been assigned to a staff position at division headquarters, Ladd AFB, near Fairbanks. We stored all our belongings, including our 1955 Mercury station wagon. We arrived on a bright sunny day and stepped out onto a dry tarmac, much to the disappointment of Barbara and the kids. They were expecting to see snow everywhere. There were no permanent quarters available for us, so we moved into a set of bachelor officer quarters (BOQs). As for snow, they soon got their wish. The temperature dropped dramatically and the snow came down in earnest. We learned there was a heated tunnel between the BOQ and the Officers' Club, which we could use to go back and forth for meals. This was very convenient but daily meals at the Club proved too expensive. So, we bought a sled. Now we could bundle up and pull two-year-old Scott to the Airmen's Mess, which was located a good distance across the base. The food was always good, and inexpensive. That was just for the evening meal. For the others, we had to improvise. We bought a few utensils and an electric frying pan. The problem was cooking in the BOQ. It was against regulations. Oh, well. The caretakers were very understanding because if one can't detect bacon frying, one has a permanently disabled sense of smell or they're dead. They did question Barbara once if she was doing any cooking there. She crossed her fingers and quietly replied, "Oh, no." They never asked again. Nice people. We cooked many great breakfasts in that Sunbeam electric frying pan that we still use to this day, nearly 60 years later.

When permanent quarters became available, we moved in and became a normal family again. We knew our first winter there would be brutal weather-wise, and that we must prepare for it. That meant parkas for Barbara and the three older kids. Barbara had them made by a local Fairbanks woman. The kids were introduced to long underwear and had to be schooled on the dangers of frostbite. Soon after we moved into quarters, I was informed that our Mercury station wagon had arrived in port at Anchorage. I had someone fly me down in a T-33. My trip back up the Richardson Highway was memorable. It was early winter. The surface of the road was covered with a thin coat of dry snow that swirled into a cloud with any disturbance. The "highway" was a two-lane winding roadway that occasionally curved around unguarded cliffs. Since I was unfamiliar with the terrain, I drove at a slower speed than normal. Trucks would pass me, and the resulting swirl of the dry snow would bring my visibility to zero. All I could do then was come off the accelerator, hold the vehicle straight ahead and hope the road ran straight. When visibility improved I would release the pucker in my butt and continue on. I started late in the afternoon, so it was going to be a long dark trip. About 2AM I noticed my headlights were dimming. The volt meter showed no charge, which meant the generator was out. It was my lucky night. I came upon a gas station that was open. When I explained my problem to the attendant, he said he knew a guy who could fix it. At this time of the morning, to my surprise, he didn't hesitate to call him. An older gentleman soon came walking into the area and introduced himself. He didn't have a replacement for the generator but did have the proper size wire that he used to rewind the armature, which took most of the rest of that night. I can't remember what he charged me, but it wasn't much. He just appeared satisfied that he was there to help. Alaskans were that way then. I hope they still are.

The Mercury station wagon had vinyl upholstery – not good in far northern temperatures. On the first below-zero morning it cracked and split in several places. Worse were the nylon tires. One day when the temperature was 57 degrees below zero, Barbara drove across the base to the commissary. The tires never became round, retaining the parked flat spot. Now that's cold! All in all, that vehicle served us well during our entire tour in cold country.

My introduction to ground operations in extreme cold conditions came when I attended a survival course, somewhere on the outskirts of Fairbanks. There was a fighter interceptor squadron stationed on base, equipped with F-89D aircraft. Their crew members were required to attend the course. Since I flew the T-33, which they used as a target for their intercept practice, I volunteered to undergo survival training with them. We were out in the wilderness for three nights with the temperatures dropping below minus-35 degrees each night. There wasn't a comfortable moment the entire time. It was a good reminder never to fly unprepared in this environment.

That winter I discovered another hazard of flying in the northern latitudes: the Aurora Borealis phenomenon. It required constant checking of your flight attitude instruments to determine your relative position in space – nose up, nose down, left turn, right turn, straight and level. Due to the constant gyrations of the Aurora, it was impossible to tell your position relative to the horizon, hence the danger of getting into an uncontrollable attitude.

Spring came, and with it came long daylight hours and short nights. There was a river that ran through the base called the Chena. To prevent large ice chunks from building up during spring thaw and causing flooding, crews would set off strategical-ly placed dynamite sticks all along this section of the river. These loud blasts had a terrible effect on Scott. He would cry until the explosions stopped and nothing or no one could settle him down. If he were susceptible to being traumatized, that would do it. In today's jargon, it would be termed Post Traumatic Stress Disorder (PTSD). But no, he turned out just fine. As spring moved into summer, the daylight hours increased to the point of no real darkness at all. Artificial darkness in the bedrooms was created by taping aluminum foil over the windows. We all re-member that one day in May 1960 when the temperature reached a record 93 degrees. Along with the heat came the mos-quito hatch. They were big, swarming, unrelenting pests that could drive unprotected human beings out of their minds. For example, a pilot ejected from a disabled T-33 right after takeoff from this base. The rescue people got to him shortly after he had touched down in his parachute. He was already frantic with mosquito swarms all over his face and neck, i.e., all his exposed skin. Beautiful Alaska has its flaws of nature, too. These pests were generally well controlled on and around the base by the liberal spraying of the pesticide DDT, both from the ground and the air.

Later that year we were informed that Ladd AFB would be turned over to the U.S. Army and be renamed Fort Wainwright. So here we go again. I contacted a friend who was the operations officer of an F-102 fighter squadron located south of us at El-mendorf AFB, near Alaska's largest city, Anchorage. They had an open position in the squadron, and he did the rest. So, in less than a year we moved again, but this time directly into base housing. No more breaking the rules with our electric frying pan. I had flown the F-102 before, so it didn't take long to learn their mission and procedures.

This squadron's mission was to defend against any hostile act committed by any Soviet air threat, part of which was located just a few miles across the Bering Strait. This threat required the deployment of fighters to different locations, two of which were in remote areas. We would spend one week on alert at these sites, keeping two airplanes and pilots on five-minute ready-alert at all times. We all pulled these alert duties except for a few who, in addition to regular flying training, had full-time duties at home base such as the Squadron Commander, the Operations Officer, and one assistant. Later, the policy changed, and the assistant would also pull alert duty. He was with my flight at our most northern alert site on his first time out. After our duty week was completed, some wild weather moved in, lowering the cloud layer to below minimums. We were not going home that night, so our new guy on alert called his wife to let her know. He later revealed to me how their conversation started. "Hi honey," he said. "Hi horny," she replied. This couple quickly became aware of some of the special ramifications of the alert schedule.

Weather was always a big factor flying in Alaska, especially in these remote areas. Flying out of our most remote airfield in mid-winter, one of our pilots experienced an engine explosion on climb-out and had to eject. We knew of an experienced Eskimo guide who lived in a village close by. When our people contacted him for help, the first thing he asked was, "What does he have on his feet?" When we told him of all the layers of foot protection we wore, he said, "He will be okay; we will find him." Within a few hours, the search party, led by this guide, found our pilot. Other than a sore back from the ejection, he was in good shape.

There were other factors to consider flying in this harsh environment, insidious factors. For example, I was making an instrument approach in a T-33 to another remote site through not more than two or three thousand feet of overcast, holding the proper airspeed throughout the approach to the point of round out for landing. When I cut the throttle for touchdown, the aircraft stalled and hit hard. Inspection shortly afterward revealed a heavy layer of ice had formed on the underside of each wing, increasing weight, which increased the stall speed considerably.

Although weather is always a challenge to flyers in Alaska, the sun shines there, too, magnifying the beauty all around, especially from 40, 000 feet. From this vantage point, the sight of a snow-covered Mt. McKinley, the Cook Inlet, and all the surrounding territories leaves me with lasting memories of natural beauty beyond description. And it goes without saying that the hunting and fishing are limitless in this wild territory, but you need an airplane to get to the good areas. Sharing the meat of wild game, salmon and trout was routine there because of the sheer volume fished and hunted by so many of us. Our large freezer was always full. Outside our front door there was a circular area in a cul-de-sac where playground equipment had been placed. Sometimes, fully grown moose would graze there in midwinter, brushing the snow aside to get at grass and roots below.

The kids had plenty of recreational activities to choose from, with skiing and ice hockey the predominant sports. When we first arrived, I built an ice rink just behind our quarters where the kids developed their skating and hockey skills. At the ages of 10 and 11, Larry was a member of a hockey team that competed throughout the city of Anchorage; he played little league baseball in the summers. All the kids did well in school and never seemed to be bored. Winters were long and, at times, bleak, and I was gone a lot. Barbara was the one who held the family together in the good times and the not so good. This wasn't new to her. Remember Korea?

Before we leave Alaska, there is one other incident I'll mention. The United States and the Soviet Union were still competing for supremacy in the Cold War. They had been testing their newly developed nuclear weapons, both underground and in the atmosphere. Negotiations to eliminate these tests in the atmosphere were ongoing and about to be signed by both sides, but the

Soviets managed to get one more test done. They exploded their largest, most powerful hydrogen blast yet, in the atmosphere over Soviet territory very near the Alaska border. I happened to be flying at that time, near 40, 000 feet. The medics were waiting for me when I landed. They tested me and the airplane with their Geiger counters. The needles on the counters went to maximum. I will always blame the damn Russians for my premature hair loss.

My tour in Alaska ended in the summer of 1962. Rather than fly out of Alaska, we decided that driving the long, rugged Alcan Highway was an adventure we should experience. I sold our Mercury wagon and bought a two-year newer Ford wagon. I also bought a small trailer to carry all the extra gear we would need for the long trip, and a small pram for lake fishing that I stacked on top of the trailer. At that time the road surface was entirely gravel, with large frost heaves thrown in for good measure. I was warned not to travel over 35 MPH on that type of surface due to heat buildup in the tires that could cause blowouts. It was good advice. Several times, drivers who had passed us would be changing wheels and tires farther on down the road. It took eight days to reach Seattle. Every day was memorable, but the Muncho Lake area stands out. We spent one night there fishing and stocking up on supplies. In winter, the locals took ice from the lake, stored it in sheds, covering it with sawdust to prevent excessive melting. That ice met our needs for several days.

The highway wound through mile after mile of uninterrupted wilderness. For adults, this could serve as a catharsis for the mind and soul. But for kids? Not so much. Looking back, I would say they handled these many hours of boredom very well. Each stop was an adventure for all of us. On one occasion, we stopped for gas and found only one man moving in the entire town – the station attendant. Apparently, there had been a big party the night before and everyone in town was hung over. All the kids liked our stop at Whitehorse, in Canada's Yukon Territory. We got in there very late and saw a light on in a building that just might be a hotel. It was, and they had one room left with just enough beds to accommodate all six of us. The toilet and showers were down the hall, a new experience for the kids.

Arriving in the Seattle area was quite a contrast to the wilderness we had traveled through for the past eight days. We continued on to Portland, stopping for a few days visit with family before driving on to my new assignment at Castle AFB near Atwater, California. This would be the 456th Fighter Interceptor Squadron, equipped with the Mach-2 capable F-106A. The airplane could be armed with air-to-air missiles and/or an atomic rocket. The mission was to destroy any incoming enemy bomber. With the atomic rocket, we also had an outside chance of destroying an incoming atomic missile. In this event, our chance of survival would be zero. In the early 1960s the Cold War was in full swing, and all options were being considered.

The F-106A was a dream to fly and capable of reaching very high altitudes. We were required to wear full pressure suits any time we exceeded 50, 000 feet. We did this many times, practicing snap-up attacks on high-flying U-2 reconnaissance planes. We never failed to get double-takes from the bomber maintenance crews as we taxied by in those moon suits. During the winter months of January through March this area of central California is submerged in a thick layer of fog. So, in order to continue flight training uninterrupted, we would deploy for days at a time to George AFB in the high desert of southern California. We also had a facility located at Edwards AFB, CA, for alert and deployment. In this line of work, there will always be family separations no matter where you happen to be stationed.

I performed many test flights which were required following major maintenance. These were flown over the Sierra Nevada mountains above 40, 000 feet because each flight required reaching Mach 2 speed. Staying over this unpopulated area minimized the effect of the resultant sonic boom. We had to reach this speed to check the operation of a system called vari-ramps, located inside the front of each air inlet. This system kept the velocity of the air reaching the engine turbine blades at sub-sonic speed. Failure of one of these ramps resulted in explosive sounds and severe engine vibration. Reducing the airspeed to subsonic was the only remedy. This happened to me several times, and on one occasion required an engine change. One day I was scheduled to take the base medical doctor for an F-106B (2 seats, tandem) orientation flight. During the pre-flight, I warned him about the possibility of the above problem. He was very talkative on the intercom during the climb to altitude. As we leveled at high altitude and began accelerating, I would read off the increasing Mach numbers to him. Just as we reached Mach 2, one of the vari-ramps failed, followed by the explosive sounds and vibration. It was out of burner, throttle to idle, and slow to subsonic. My talkative passenger was silent for the remainder of the flight, and I wondered about the color of his underwear.

Our family soon adjusted to the new house and neighborhood, associated expense of such, and work required for upkeep. There was plenty of the latter. There were large back and side yards which required workup for planting grass, establishing a vegetable garden, and setting up posts for clothes lines. Automatic clothes dryers were still in the future for us. Our new grass yard attracted moles, lots of moles. Our great house cat quickly reduced their population. He always seemed to need praise for his stealthy accomplishments. If Barbara happened to be out hanging laundry on the clothes lines, the cat would proudly lay his latest kill at her feet. What a show-off!

The kids made great friends in the neighborhood. The two oldest, Michelle and Larry, landed their first regular paying jobs, working on weekends and holidays in a peach and apricot processing area, cutting and pitting the fruit to ready it for dry-ing in sulfur ovens. They still look back on how much they hated their first paying job. Of course, I told them "It builds character." When Michelle turned 15, she got her learners permit to drive. After that, she would be outside waiting for her evening driving lesson every day when I got home. At that time, her younger brother Larry was excelling in Little League baseball, getting more print in the local newspaper than the mayor of little Atwater. Renee and Scott were fortunate to have friends their age to play with, some of whom were poor Mexican immigrant families whose sons later joined our military and fought in the Viet Nam War. It was a great neighborhood to raise a family, located in the middle of California's San Joaquin Valley, an agricultural breadbasket with tremendous quantities and varieties of fruits, nuts, and vegetables.

The Cuban Missile Crisis in 1962 caused rumbles throughout the military. Troops were being deployed and redeployed, fighter and bomber squadrons were being dispersed here and there, which gave most of us the impression of knee-jerk response or high-level incompetence. It turned out that neither was the case. High-flying U-2 reconnaissance planes had photographed ballistic missile sites under construction on Cuban soil. Both sides were serious, which meant the use of nuclear weapons was a definite possibility. Fortunately for the whole world, the Soviets finally blinked, dismantled the missile sites, and the crisis cooled.

The situation had little effect on our squadron. We deployed just 30 miles south to the Fresno airport for that short duration.

While with the squadron at Castle AFB there were a couple of flights I'd like to forget. The commander of Air Defense Command (ADC) in Colorado Springs was hosting a conference that included top brass and civilian dignitaries from Washington, DC. Our commander was tasked to lead a commemorative fly-over consisting of our four F-106 aircraft, followed in trail by a flight each of F-101s, F-102s, and F-104s. I was asked to fly in the back seat of the F-106B that the ADC commander would be flying to lead the formation. That day there was a dense haze over the entire area. The airfield was completely obscured at the lower altitudes. We lined up with the flights in trail and flew inbound toward the field. What I didn't know was that my pilot (our CO) didn't have the field in sight. The closer he got without sighting the field, the more he would come back on the throttle. Since I had flown the F-104, I knew their stalling speed was higher than ours, so I put my hand on the throttle in the rear to prevent him from further reducing our airspeed. I didn't realize in time that he was in panic mode, or I would have suggested he bring the formation around and track inbound to and from the ground radio homer, just like in a normal instrument approach. I guess he thought, since I was back there, I should have given him a heads up. Since he hadn't uttered a word, I assumed he had the field in sight. He didn't. We missed flying over or even near the field, and by then the "formation" had become nothing more than a few airplanes flying in the same general direction. In short, a total embarrassment. I should have reacted sooner, rather than sit there like a lump until it was too late.

Shortly after this episode, the second flight-to-forget occurred. A team of five pilots and maintenance personnel deployed to Tyndall AFB, located at Panama City, Florida, to compete in a missile-firing competition. I was one of the pilots. The targets would be remote-controlled drones flying several miles off the coast of the Gulf of Mexico. Two pilots would be strapped into the cockpits of their fighters on the parking ramp, waiting for scramble orders. The competition required each pilot of each team to lead flights in rotation throughout the exercise. This was a night mission using infrared missiles. I was lead pilot on this one, with the squadron commander scrambling off behind me and following by his own radar approximately five miles in trail. The ground radar controller directed me toward the drone, and just before I locked onto the target, the controller yelled, "Break it off, break it off hard." That meant throttle idle and straight down to me, assuming there was a heat-seeking missile coming up my ass. That's what I did, and that's what it was. Number Two had locked onto my aircraft instead of the drone and fired. It was close. I don't remember whether he even bought me a beer for that screw-up.

While we were with the squadron at Castle AFB, I was promoted to Major. That meant I should assume a position of greater responsibility there or move on. The latter happened. A strange thing occurred while I was still assigned here. One day while sitting in the fighter lounge, I was asked to come to the administration office. The sergeant there showed me a directive he had received from headquarters. Due to my time AWOL in November 1943, my retirement date would be set ahead three days. This was when I took off to see my brother at his base in Muroc, CA. And remember, I was in the Navy then. Someone was digging deep into my past for some reason. I never found out why.

We packed up and moved on down the road to Norton AFB near the city of San Bernardino, California. I had been reassigned to an operations staff position at the Los Angeles Air Defense Sector at Norton. We rented a newly constructed house in north San Bernardino. The kids quickly assimilated. Michelle started high school here at Pacific High, which had the largest student body in the nation at that time. What a shock it was for her, following her small-town school experience in Atwater. Larry attended a junior high school nearby where he excelled academically and played on the school's basketball and football teams. When summer came, he was back on the baseball diamond, this time with the pony league, pitching strikeouts and hitting balls over the scoreboard. Renee in the sixth grade and Scott in the second attended school a short distance from our house.

While we were living in Atwater I had purchased an old wreck of a Chevrolet to get me back and forth to work. This time I bought an Austin-Healy Sprite. It was old, small, compact and had four on the floor. This set-up was new to Michelle, so she decided to wait until later in life to get acquainted with a stick and a clutch. Barbara was kept very busy organizing the new house, the yard, the kids and everything else that comes along with the moving nightmare. We still had the 17-inch black and white TV we bought just before I left for Korea. One of our new neighbors saw it during his first visit with us and said, "That's got to go." Fixing TV sets was a hobby for him, and he had several in his garage. He brought over a color model the next day and out went our old, trusty black-and-white.

The top boss at my new assignment had been the commander at the Yuma, Arizona base when we practiced aerial gunnery there years before. So, he knew me. He had become a brigadier general, and the rule at that time was generals never fly alone. Since he was current in the F-106 and I was the only other pilot in the building also still current, I became his designated pilot in the back seat. That arrangement turned out well for me. For one thing, it got me out of the building; and, during those travels I became privy to some firsthand information. For example, we landed once at Wright Patterson AFB in Dayton, Ohio, and were given a tour of the recently developed, giant C-5 transport aircraft. This particular airplane was set up with bunks all through the cargo bay to demonstrate its ability to evacuate large numbers of wounded from the battle area. As we left the hanger, the general leaned over near me and said, "If they start carrying nurses on these things, somebody will get in trouble." That's not exactly how he put it, but close. He had flown many combat missions in both the European and Pacific theaters in World War II, early in the Korean War, and very early in the Viet Nam War. One night we landed late at a base near Kansas City, Missouri. We went to the Officers' Club dining area for dinner. They said, "We're closed, General, but we'll get you something anyway." If you're in Kansas City, what do you eat? Big, fat steaks, of course. And that's what they brought us, the most delicious I've ever tasted. After a couple of martinis and that big steak, we started telling war stories. I mostly listened. Fascinating tales.

I had a friend at that time who was flying for Air America in Southeast Asia. He kept writing and suggesting that I join them there. This organization was part of the CIA. I mentioned this to my boss, the general, because he probably knew anyone of consequence involved. A short time later I received a call from someone in Washington, D.C. He identified himself, asked a lot of questions, and said he would get back to me. A few months went by before I heard from him again. In the meantime, I had been selected for advancement to the rank of Lieutenant Colonel, to take effect in a couple of months. The one-sided telephone call went like this, "Call me when you're ready to go." Having passed muster with the CIA, it was now decision time. If I retired then, it would be as a Major and the promotion goes out the window. I stayed in and never heard another word from the CIA contact. My friend in Southeast Asia was later killed in a mid-air collision over an airport near Vientiane, Laos.

The Los Angeles Air Defense Sector headquarters closed in 1966, and I was assigned to Headquarters Western Air Defense Force located at, you guessed it, Hamilton AFB. Barbara and the kids remained in San Bernardino to finish out the school year. I went north and lived in the BOQ, traveling back and forth on weekends via T-33. Once we were together again, and after living a short period in a rental in town, we moved into quarters on base. I had so many memories of the action on and around this base. Here are a few examples. Before receiving Northrop Aviation's F-89 into the squadron, Bill Lear, designer of the autopilot we would be using (and later the Learjet passenger plane), stopped by in his own twin-engine Cessna. He gave a few of us a flight demonstration, using his autopilot for low visibility approaches. He was quite a character. In another event, the fighter group did a mass flyover for the dedication of the newly completed Shasta Dam in Northern California. We all tried especially hard to make it look perfect because we expected President Truman to be there, observing. We later found out that he hadn't made it. No big surprise. He was the President after all, and just might have had something more important to do that day than watch us fly over a dam. There were accidents, too, and a bad one happened a few months after my first assignment there. I was on duty in the base operations office near the flight line when a flight of three F-84Ds were on the takeoff roll in formation. The two wingmen rotated and took off, but the lead aircraft aborted late and crashed into the dike at the end of the runway. I jumped in the ops vehicle and headed to the crash. An Air Police guard was just coming off duty from the base perimeter. We met at the crash scene. The pilot had jettisoned his canopy and was trying to exit the cockpit when the airplane exploded into a huge fireball. We both tried to get to him, but the fire was too hot. I will always remember the Air policeman standing back from the flames, tears streaming down his face.

Being assigned to a headquarters sometimes had its perks. A call came in from higher headquarters asking for two volunteers to ferry an armed T-33 to Bogota, Colombia, for use by their government forces against the rebels. I was then back in the tactical evaluation business, and my boss volunteered the two of us. We picked up the airplane at a base in southern Texas. Considering the availability of jet fuel, our flight plan took us to Mexico City, Managua, and Bogota. Mexican military troops met us at the airplane and looked it over thoroughly to make sure the guns weren't armed. They then escorted us to the terminal entrance, holding out their hands for the expected bribe to enter the area. Even though neither of us understood the language, we quickly got the message and complied. We spent the night and took off the next day, landing at a civilian airport in Managua. We spent the night there at a very nice hotel. We had an excellent dinner that night at the upstairs dining room, all the while being entertained by a very accomplished black jazz pianist, who happened to be an American and a very interesting individual.

The last leg of the journey to Bogota was the most interesting because of imperfect, intermittent reception from ground navigation equipment. Our reliance on old fashioned time-and-distance ground navigation techniques paid off. The approach and landing alone was a butt puckerer. Runway elevation there is 12, 000 feet, which means the aircraft stall speed is higher than it is near sea level. So, if you carry too much speed over the fence and touch down long, the runway gets too short real fast. We walked away from it, which means it was a good landing. We were met by a military group that immediately took possession of the aircraft. We went into the lounge area and found a long bar serving free Columbian coffee. I thought, "It figures, that's what they're noted for." It was strong, and it was delicious. I had a friend who was on duty as a military attaché there in Bogota. He picked us up and took us to our hotel. This was a civilian airport, but there were armed military guards on duty at the exit. The country was in turmoil dealing with communist insurgents and drug cartels.

That night we went to my friend's house for cocktails and dinner. I found out quickly that more than one martini at that altitude is something to avoid. We didn't exactly make asses of ourselves, but I'm sure our end of the conversation was less than charming.

The trip back by commercial airliner proved to be a disaster simply because they made a stop at Mexico City. The delay there was to be about an hour, and all passengers were allowed to visit the terminal. Somehow, we took a wrong turn and ended up outside the waiting area. Getting back meant we had to grease the palm of a guard at the entrance to the waiting area. Neither of us had any cash, so the airplane took off without us. We later convinced one of these crooks to take a check, and we were allowed back into the boarding area to wait for the next available flight. We left with a bad impression of life directly south of our border.

Scotty leads a formation of F-106s over Lake Tahoe. Part of this mission was to take this picture for use as a postcard.

*Author talking with Senator Henry "Scoop" Jackson
following their flight in a T-33.*

SKETCHES OF AN EARLIER TIME

Part 6

The Vietnam War

In the fall of 1967 I received orders for an assignment in Southeast Asia. This came as no surprise. The war had been escalating since we became fully involved there in the early 1960s. My immediate boss and I received identical orders, but first we had to get checked out and become fully familiar with another fighter aircraft, the F-4D Phantom. This fighter was designed for both air-to-air and air-to-ground combat. It was also capable of reaching Mach 2 speed, a neighborhood I was becoming very familiar with. The training center for this airplane and the F-105 was at George AFB, located in the upper desert about 40 miles northeast of San Bernardino. George was an ideal training base. It had two long concrete runways, two firing ranges located in an isolated area of the Mojave Desert, and a long emergency landing area in the desert at nearby Edwards AFB. We spent about a month there, getting acquainted with both its air-to-air and air-to-ground capabilities. When our training was completed, I went back to Hamilton Field to face another move. Barbara and the kids could not live on base while I was overseas; it was considered a permanent change of station, even though they couldn't accompany me, just like Korea. So once again, we settled in nearby Novato.

I left for Thailand shortly after Christmas, 1967. This time, rather than sailing under it, I flew west, over the Golden Gate Bridge. When I arrived in Saigon I immediately transferred to a C-130 cargo airplane for the final leg of the trip to an airbase near Nakhon Phanom, typically shortened to NKP, or as many Americans there called it, Naked Fanny. This base was located near the Mekong River and about 200 miles northeast of Bangkok. It had one runway with a large ramp area for parking and maintaining a unit of O-2 aircraft. It supported forward air control (FAC) missions, a squadron of A-1 single reciprocating engine aircraft for general purpose missions along the Ho Chi Minh Trail, a squadron of helicopters, and a U.S. Navy squadron of P-2 Neptunes. In addition, there was a contingent of U.S. Army Special Operations troops located there who were doing just that – special operations. For example, a C-130 painted totally black – no markings – would land in the middle of the night, load up with Thai fighters led by our special ops troops, take off, and not be seen again for days. I met one of their officers one night at the bar we had in the mess hall. The next day he gave me a tour of his area. I couldn't get much information from him except for his saying that occasionally they would lose a few folks in some extremely brutal manner.

My job at NKP turned out to be very different from what I expected. I worked in a very modern, newly constructed building loaded with the latest computer equipment and programmed for this mission. We were attempting to stop or disrupt the human and motorized traffic coming down the Ho Chi Minh Trail. To accomplish this, we employed listening and movement detection devices. The double and triple-canopy trees along the Trail made it virtually impossible to observe any movement with the human eye. These detection devices, or sensors, were known as ADSIDS, ACOBOUYS, and SPIKEBOUYS.

When I arrived, the Navy Neptunes and helicopters were delivering the sensors. In addition, the A-1 aircraft would drop small pellets of explosives, termed GRAVEL, along the Trail to blow tires and inflict injuries on marchers. The detection devices would relay any sound or movement to computers installed in C-121 aircraft flying overhead 24/7, which would then send the information back to the computers in our main building. We then had the option to call in an immediate strike or, in the case of a truck park, suggest a strike in the near future. Here is an example. This happened when the TET offensive of 1968 was in full force. Our Marines were involved in a full-scale battle at Khe Sanh. We notified them that there were several tanks heading their way. Their reply, "They don't have tanks." Our reply, "Believe us, these are tanks." They believed us, knocked them all out, and later sent us a gift: a Russian-made truck filled with every type of maintenance equipment for fixing their supply trucks broken down on the Trail. To a trained operator in the computer center, the ground sensors would show speed, direction, and in many cases, type. In this case, the operator was dead right.

Another incident involved an ACOBOUY. This one was dropped in the trees above a truck park. They were equipped with tiny microphones. One of the enemy troops had found one and was taking it apart. What came through back at our computer room, translated in English, went like this, "Just like those F---ing Americans. There's nothing in it." Once a truck park like this was discovered, fighter strikes could be directed to those coordinates, pinpointed by rockets fired by a forward air controller, and struck with whatever ordinance was required. Secondary explosions following the strike indicated a successful sensor placement.

I flew many missions with the FACs in their O-2 Cessna aircraft. On the very first one, we were over a known hot area when 37mm shells started breaking around us. I recognized them from Korea. The pilot said, "I think we should get out of here." I agreed, but that doesn't happen very fast in a Cessna. In a jet at 400 MPH-plus, you break away and you're out of there. In the Cessna, when you're being shot at flying at 150 MPH, it feels like you're hovering, waiting to take a hit. Not only did these FAC pilots mark targets, they covered downed fighter pilots and other aircrews during rescue operations. They earned their flight pay.

The Navy P-2 had been dropping these sensors since the beginning of the war. The enemy would see the P-2s fly over and fly away with no follow-on explosions, so why shoot at them and reveal their position? That was the apparent thinking until one day they decided, it's the enemy, it can't be good; let's shoot it down. And they did. Each P-2 carried a crew of nine. There was no laughter at the bar that night. Then a few days later they shot another one down. That ended this part of the Navy's mission in Southeast Asia. The U.S. Air Force would expedite deployment of the F-4D Squadron (training for this mission in Florida) to the USAF airbase at Ubon, Thailand. I was there when they arrived. They had flown non-stop, with several air refueling hookups en route. As they parked and cut their engines, one could sense the long-awaited easing of tension, of both the aircraft and the crews inside.

Back to Naked Fanny. One day I was flying with a FAC over a known enemy gun emplacement area called Chapone. He wanted to show me where he had covered a downed F-4 pilot. We were down low, circling the area for some time. As we left, the rear engine sputtered and died. The other engine couldn't sustain flight, so we prepared for bailout. Then we spotted an open area that appeared to be a perfect place for an emergency landing. We alerted the home field, who in turn alerted rescue.

By then, we are lining up for landing. The field wasn't the way it appeared from altitude, not even close. It was nothing but rocks and brush. Just before touchdown I noticed that the pilot didn't have his shoulder harness locked. I grabbed him the best I could to keep his face from hitting the windscreen. There is only one door on this airplane, on the passenger side. It was jammed when we came to a skidding stop. I braced myself against the pilot's seat and kicked the door open with both feet. I see armed people on the immediate horizon who don't look friendly. They are all looking skyward at several heavily armed A-1 airplanes with call sign "Sandy" whose pilots are trained for just this purpose. One of our own helicopters touched down in short order about a hundred yards from us. We ran like hell for the chopper. He dove in first with me following, scrambling in next to the door gunner. We made it back across the Mekong River to NKP with no further problems. This part of Laos (where we left our plane) was hotly contested. One day the good guys had it, the next day the bad. One day when we controlled it, a heavy helicopter with salvage crew was sent in to recover the wreck and bring it back to NKP. That's when we learned that a small arms bullet had punctured the gas line to the engine.

With the new squadron of F-4s now operational at Ubon and dedicated to the sensor laying mission, I thought my fighter flying days would finally begin again. That wasn't to be. The headquarters folks in Saigon would allow me only minimal time and only in the back seat. So be it. I took what I could get. Here is an example of how they delivered ADSIDS: Line up with a stretch of open Trail 500 feet above the ground traveling at 500 knots, release and let the preset electronics determine the spacing. The pilot in back flies the airplane as if on instruments. This method made a more precise sensor ground pattern, and that speed and altitude greatly reduced the chance of being hit by ground fire. But these were F-4s, capable of carrying multiple munitions and performing multiple missions. On one flight, after completing a sensor drop mission, we were directed to hit a target not far from our drop. We were carrying CBU-24s (cluster bombs). The ground fire became visible immediately after our roll in on the target. After climbing back to altitude and leveling off, I mentioned that this was my third war with people shooting at my ass. He let me fly it home, enjoying myself with a few acrobatics on the way, and then making the landing from the back seat. Each pilot I flew with after that did the same; word must have gotten around.

There was an area in the Trail that presented a choke point for interdiction at a place called Ban Phenop (sp). The combat planners developed a mission of non-stop bombing in this area that continued for three days and nights. Our General had been to headquarters in Saigon arguing against this plan due to the known persistence of the enemy. He wanted to prove his point. While the bombing was underway, we intercepted this two-way message. "Suffering many losses. Advise." The answer came back, "Bury your dead and continue." The general needed more evidence. At our morning briefing I told him I would get him some pictures. I checked out a hand-held camera, got a FAC assigned, and we took off for the area. When we got there, I took pictures of them climbing up over the karst (high jagged rocks) and back to the Trail beyond the bombed-out area. They were a most determined enemy.

Occasionally, we got the opportunity for R&R. When we would take two or three days off and go to Bangkok, we would stay in a hotel leased by our government for use by American and allied forces. It was called The Chow Piya. That's as close as I can come to the spelling. Due to the clandestine nature of much of the war, this place stood out as a stopping-off place for people involved in top-secret action all over the Southeast Asia area of operations. In fact, all the operations out of NKP were just that. So, going to the bar was an adventure in itself. You might be talking to a CIA spook, an Air America pilot, or a Special Forces troop, all in Bangkok for a break from the tension of their war. The bar itself was dimly lit, giving off an atmosphere of intrigue unlike any I have ever experienced. It was kind of like the bar in the World War II movie, *Casablanca*, without the piano player.

Scotty and his O-2 pilot exiting from the rescue helicopter that returned them to the base at NKP.

Part 7

The Later Years

O ur tour of duty at NKP was up in December 1968. We left by military transport aircraft out of Saigon and landed at Travis AFB, California, which is several miles due east of Hamilton AFB. I got a ride to Novato where lots of hugs from Barbara and the kids made for a warm welcome home. Then we packed again for our next move. I had been assigned to the Air Force Safety Center Headquarters located at Norton AFB, back in the San Bernardino area. I became current in the F-106 again, and in the T-39 twin engine jet transport aircraft. I was later assigned head of the fighter division. Following my promotion to Colonel, I was assigned responsibility for the entire flight safety division.

On many occasions we were required to observe and assist in the onsite investigation of an aircraft accident. For example, a C-130 cargo aircraft crashed through a forest of pine trees in North Carolina, throwing debris everywhere and leaving no survivors. In another accident, a T-38 crashed on takeoff from a Texas base with a senior ranking general officer and his aide on board – no survivors. In the best year during my tour in Safety there were

200 major accidents. Bad, but a far cry from World War II years when they could get as high as 1400 accidents in one month.

The safety job wasn't entirely gloomy. The Taiwanese Air Force requested through channels that we send a team to inspect the operations of some of their flying squadrons, from a safety standpoint. Their squadrons were all equipped with American airplanes like C-119 cargo planes and F-100 fighters. I led teams on two different trips. It's a 14-hour flight from the West Coast to Taipei. We were picked up at the airport by an English-speaking Chinese officer who would be our guide and interpreter. Early the following morning I was awakened by telephone, given a message that the General will see me, and that I would be picked up in thirty minutes, leaving little time to adjust to the time change. We got along well, and I would brief him at the end of the inspection.

On this trip we traveled to the opposite end of the island to inspect an F-100 fighter wing. We were flown there on a C-47 cargo plane which had been converted to a plush passenger airplane. The crew included a beautiful hostess who kept us supplied with goodies all the way. The inspection went as expected. They really weren't up to our standards. For example, we had them put a pilot in the cockpit of an F-100 with the canopy closed. We told them he had just gone off the end of the runway, he was unconscious, and the airplane was on fire. They were all over and around the airplane, chattering constantly with no one in charge. It must have been 10-15 minutes before they got the pilot (simulating unconsciousness) out of the airplane. One of our guys came up to me when it was over and asked, "What do you think." I couldn't resist saying, "It looked like a Chinese fire drill to me."

The Wing Commander invited me to visit him at his headquarters. He proudly showed me what he used for transportation: a beautifully restored, early World War II Jeep. He asked if I would like to drive it. Of course, I accepted. I drove it around the compound a couple of times, thinking how much I would like to own this historic icon. Our interpreter later remarked what an honor that was; apparently, only that commander had ever driven that Jeep. When the inspection was over, we prepared the critique, which I delivered through an interpreter the following day in a huge auditorium with every member of the Wing in attendance. I had to tell them they didn't do very well, but also how we thought they could improve. Despite the bad news, it was well received. They took our comments and recommendations seriously and invited us back two more times in later years.

In preparing to leave Taiwan, they arranged for the same C-47 to take us back to Taipei. I demurred, saying we would like to experience the sights of their beautiful countryside by returning by train. At boarding time, we were all very thirsty and headed directly to the club car for an ice-cold beer. The action for the past week had been intense, and the beers were going down as fast as the back-and-forth stories were being told. After several rounds, the waiter came back with bad news: we had drunk them out of beer. Our interpreter talked the engineer into stopping at a small village to replenish the supply, but there was none to be had. I guess there is a first time for everything. We had been eating local food for the past week, leaving us all hungry for an American hamburger. We got these at the Officers' Club in downtown Taipei. Soon afterwards we all got throw-up sick.

After getting back to Norton AFB, we resumed our normal routine, monitoring flight safety problems all over the globe. I had three bosses during my tour here. The first was the General I flew with in the F-106B when I was with the Los Angeles Air Defense Sector. Next was the Colonel, now General, who had led the 8th Tactical fighter wing at Ubon, Thailand, just prior to my visits there. Third and last was then General Yeager, the first to break the sound barrier years earlier. All three of these men were very knowledgeable, combat-experienced officers capable of commanding at the highest level. But, that didn't happen, which surprised me. Too bad, our loss.

Flying the T-39 small transport jet was a new experience for me. It looked like a fighter with passenger seats, six or eight as I recall. It was made by North American Aviation, the same company that designed and manufactured the F-86. The feel of that fighter was all around you, swept wings and all. I flew hundreds of hours in the T-39 and enjoyed the experience. In one flight I will always remember, I was flying from Andrews AFB in Washington, DC, with a planned stop for refueling at Tinker AFB in Oklahoma City. The passenger seats were full. For some reason, traffic control directed me to descend to a lower altitude much earlier than planned, which was fine if the weather would be as briefed. It wasn't. Thunderstorm activity forms rapidly in this area, and Oklahoma City was surrounded by massive thunderstorms. When I notified the FAA controller of my fuel situation, and that I wasn't equipped with radar for navigating around the bad spots in the storm, the captain of a commercial airliner broke in, identified his company and tail number, and said, "Put him in trail with me. We'll take him through." And they did, transmitting compass directions that would keep me directly in trail of the airliner. We flew through very heavy rain and almost constant lightning flashes with a cabin full of non-aviator type passengers, all with white knuckles. Despite all that weather, we encountered only slight turbulence on the aircraft. When we broke through, I said, "Thanks, not a ripple."

My tour ended there in 1973. I had received word through the personnel grapevine that I was being considered for a fighter command slot in Europe. It didn't happen. I found that some Colonel in the Pentagon had talked his way into that slot. I was assigned instead to be the senior advisor to the New York Air National Guard, stationed at the Suffolk County Air Base just outside Westhampton Beach on Long Island, NY. We packed up the car and headed east. Michelle, Larry and Renee were either finished with college, in the middle of it, or about to enter. Our youngest, Scott, drove out with us and continued high school there. I retired at the end of that assignment, in October of 1975, and we moved back to the West Coast.

Final Thoughts

This has been a long journey for me, recalling and reliving experiences of my first 50 years. The depression years affected a substantial percentage of the American people. For the most part, they were a proud and capable part of society, reluctant to accept handouts. For example, our local grocery store held charge accounts for those down on their luck. We were one of those families. I remember the day vividly when, following a long unproductive period, my dad finally found work and paid off our whopping $40 grocery bill. Now that, my friends, is the meaning of the words stress and relief. This scenario was duplicated all over the country.

The years leading up to our country's involvement in World War II must have been extremely worrisome for the older folks. They read, heard on the radio, and yes, watched via Movie Tone News in theaters the news of the fighting in Europe and the gross atrocities being perpetrated by the Japanese in China. They knew that the United States involvement could not be far off and that their sons would be called upon to defend our allies in their fight for survival and, in the long run, our own. When it happened, they demonstrated to the enemy and the world what free people can accomplish when forced to relinquish their youth to battle. I think, without doubt, the rapidly developed capability to produce vast quantities of war materials was unprecedented in the history of warfare – anywhere! Our losses were high but think about how much higher they would have been if not for the commitment of almost every U.S. citizen to the war effort.

Some years back I read a statistic that surprised me. It stated that of all the U.S. military members organized to fight World War II, only 10 percent were involved in actual combat. Though part of a small minority, every combat veteran knows that without the incredible dedication of all the support personnel and civilians turning out the massive amount of required equipment and supplies where and when we needed them, it is impossible to determine today what the outcome would have been.

The two follow-on wars of my time, in Korea and Vietnam, were undeclared by our Congress and, compared to World War II, significantly undersold to the American people. As wars with the compelling purpose to stop the spread of communist ideology and totalitarian government in distant places, they were not treated with the same level of seriousness and commitment by political commentators, the news media in general, nor certainly academia. A few standout American leaders at the time, like Senator Henry "Scoop" Jackson, advocated strongly to counter these threats to free people everywhere. In the end, it wasn't enough.

The military wins the battles, but actual victory cannot be achieved without the collective and continuing will and support of the people, especially a free people.

Finally, as I bring this personal memoir to an end, I would like to extend my heartfelt appreciation and downright love for all the troops manning the battle stations today. And that goes double for their families at home.

Made in the USA
Las Vegas, NV
30 July 2023

75437071R00088